August Strindberg

Routledge Modern and
Contemporary Dramatists

Eszter Szalczer

Routledge
Taylor & Francis Group

LONDON AND NEW YORK

First published 2011
by Routledge
2 Park Square, Milton Park, Abingdon, Oxon OX14 4RN

Simultaneously published in the USA and Canada
by Routledge
270 Madison Avenue, New York, NY 10016

*Routledge is an imprint of the Taylor & Francis Group, an
informa business*

Typeset in Sabon by Taylor & Francis Books
Printed and bound in Great Britain by TJ International Ltd,
Padstow, Cornwall

British Library Cataloguing in Publication Data
A catalogue record for this book is available from the British
Library

Library of Congress Cataloging in Publication Data
Szalczer, Eszter.
    August Strindberg / Eszter Szalczer.
      p. cm. – (Routledge modern and contemporary dramatists)
    Includes bibliographical references and index.
    1. Strindberg, August, 1849–1912–Criticism and
interpretation. 2. Strindberg, August, 1849–1912–Dramatic
production. 3. Strindberg, August, 1849–1912–Stage history.
I. Title.
    PT9816.S93 2010
    839.72'6 – dc22
                                        2010009723

ISBN 13: 978-0-415-41422-7 (hbk)
ISBN 13: 978-0-415-41423-4 (pbk)
ISBN 13: 978-0-203-85288-0 (ebk)

Contents

Illustrations

Acknowledgements

I would like to acknowledge the generous support I received throughout the course of this study. An extended research period in the summer and fall of 2007 was made possible by the American National Endowment for the Humanities Summer Stipend and a sabbatical granted by the University at Albany, State University of New York. The archives of the Strindberg Museum in Stockholm and Sigtuna Foundation in Sigtuna, Sweden provided a rich treasury of source materials. My research benefited from the assistance of friends and colleagues, including Erik Höök at the Strindberg Museum and Marie-Louise Jaensson at the Intimate Theatre in Stockholm, and I owe special thanks to Birgitta Steene, Anita Persson, Yuu Komaki, Dana Marouf, Karen Knape, and Tamás Szalczer. I am grateful for the guidance, readings, and painstaking editorial comments of Maggie Gale and Mary Luckhurst and to Michael Robinson for his trust in me. My thanks to Ben Piggott at Routledge for helping me through the process.

Unless otherwise indicated, translations from the Swedish are mine.

This book is dedicated to the memory of my father, Miklós Kiss.

ES

Overview

Johan August Strindberg (1849–1912) – dramatist, theatre practitioner, novelist, painter, and essayist – was above all one of the most radical innovators of the modern theatre. His writing, including some sixty plays written between 1869 and 1909, takes up some seventy volumes in the current Swedish national edition of his collected works. But in spite of countless attempts to grasp the person behind his extensive creative output, Strindberg remains a theatre artist whose image persistently overshadows our perception of his work, and he keeps eluding us behind the personae assumed by or projected on his ever-antagonising figure. In his native country,Sweden, for example, he earned the reputation of rebel and troublemaker, while at the same time he was hailed by the new wave of modernist writers as a great innovator and renewer of the Swedish language. He appears simultaneously as a fervent social critic rebelling against any given political, religious, or cultural authority and as a reactionary ideologue in regard to women's liberation. One of the more immediate motivating forces behind Strindberg's efforts to reform and renew drama and theatre was his profound dissatisfaction with the commercial theatre of his time. But in a wider context, the common denominator to his often contradictory views and diverse activities emerges from a restless drive to find adequate expression for his sense of an elusive reality and changing culture as *fin-de-siècle* Europe entered the era of modernity.

The third child among seven of shipping merchant Carl Oscar Strindberg and former waitress Ulrika Eleonora Norling, August

Strindberg was born in a moderately well-to-do upper-middle-class family on 22 January 1849 in Stockholm, Sweden. But the circumstances of his childhood were shrouded in myth that Strindberg constructed in numerous texts. His autobiographical novel, *The Maidservant's Son* (1886), for example, presents Johan, its plebeian protagonist, as an unwanted child born in the midst of the father's bankruptcy (Strindberg 1966b: 15). This legend of his youth underpins the entire oeuvre, which in several versions elaborates the role of the playwright as a seeker of truth, an outcast and a scapegoat. Ishmael, Job, and the Flying Dutchman are but a few of those roles in which the author casts himself in the pages of his autobiographical writings. But Strindberg research, including the classic works of Swedish scholars Martin Lamm and Gunnar Brandell, has paid much attention to unravelling factual information about the author's life, which today is still often seen as the basis of his writing. In contrast to an uncomplicated biographical approach, this volume explores the complex and often deliberately ambiguous interplay between life and fiction, the person and his personae, which infiltrates Strindberg's texts. Rather than vainly attempting to uncover the biographical individual behind the author's masks, the present study proposes to understand him as a metamorphic character in his own ubiquitous play.

Such all-encompassing theatricality, as we shall see in the following chapters, is the most characteristic expression of Strindberg's modernity. As he experienced the dissolution of conventional class, gender, and family-roles, he introduced the notion of the 'characterless' character in the preface to his play *Miss Julie* (1888). Here he claims that the figures of his drama are modern 'souls' because they are split, vacillating, and lack stable identities. Thus the 'multiplicity of motives' that Strindberg deploys to support the actions of his characters is 'in keeping with the times' in its departure from the

> middle-class expression for an automaton, so that an individual whose nature had once and for all set firm or adapted to a certain role in life, who had stopped growing, in short, was called a character, whereas someone who goes on developing,

the skilful navigator on the river of life ... was called characterless.

(Strindberg 1998: 58–59)

In this and many later texts Strindberg plays with the conception of character as a series of fleeting roles. He goes even further when he puts himself on the 'stage' of his texts in the guise of his characters, and makes the dramatist both the actor and the spectator of the action. He does this through a deliberately auto-biographical framing of his plays, which consists of hints and references to his life. Again, *Miss Julie* provides a fitting example, where the aristocratic protagonist could easily be identified with Strindberg's first wife, the baroness Siri von Essen, and the valet Jean with Strindberg, a 'maidservant's son'. The point of the drama, however, is not to give snippets of the author's personal life, but rather, to convincingly represent on stage the lived experience. In other words, it is not the facts of the dramatist's life that are foregrounded in Strindberg's plays (we do not need to know Strindberg's biography to understand them), but the staging of an experience from the point of view of the experiencing consciousness. As one of Strindberg's many writer alter-egos notes in the late novel, *Black Banners* (1904), 'it seemed to me from an early age that my life was staged before me so that I would be able to observe all its facets. This insight made me reconcile with misfortune and taught me to consider myself an object' (Strindberg 1995: 147). This remark reveals a deeply paradoxical relationship to both reality and writing. Through writing the author turns his life into a laboratory experiment, where the scientist and the 'guinea pig' are one and the same person, exposing the split consciousness of the observer/manipulator and the suffering victim. Thus, while Strindberg's dramatic writing draws heavily upon the personal experience of the author's life-events amidst a culture in transition, a single-handedly biographical reading of the plays misses his most vital contribution: his role in dramatising the experience of modernity by turning a life he knew best – his own – into theatre.

Part I of this study ('Versions of a life') sets out to untangle the complex narrative that Strindberg constructed, in which myth and politics merge to shape the image of a life. Strindberg's own auto-biographical position is assessed in the light of his evolving political and artistic allegiances and that of his avowed tendency to myth-making and play-acting. Rather than the factual details of a life, what emerges from this approach is a 'performance' of a life by means of which Strindberg grappled with the artistic and political dilemmas of the transitional times he lived through. This section also aims to navigate the reader through the pitfalls and contra-dictions of the immense body of Strindberg criticism. Traditional approaches are juxtaposed with more recent re-evaluations in an attempt to show how the figure of the playwright has been variously 'shaped' historically and critically.

Part II ('A life in the theatre') then focuses on Strindberg's thea-trical achievements, his experimental theories and practices, in the context of historical events and cultural influences. Strindberg's diverse dramatic output, which profoundly affected the direction of European theatre, embodies a quintessentially modernist sensibility. At the waning of the nineteenth century he emerged as one of the leading figures of the first wave of modern dramatists, along with Ibsen, Chekhov, Shaw, and Wilde. Part of the irony surrounding his achievement is that some of his most ground-breaking works were hailed with enthusiasm and produced abroad long before they were performed in Sweden. The political controversies and the love–hate relationship with his homeland forced Strindberg into voluntary exile abroad in 1893, with brief interruptions, for some fifteen years, most notably in Berlin (1892–94) and Paris (1894–97). His outlook was tremendously informed by his experiencing at first hand the rapidly changing life and cultural ferment in these modern capitals and by being part of intellectual circles (including Norwe-gian painter Edvard Munch, Polish decadent author Stanislaw Przybyszewski, and the French artist Paul Gauguin) that rebelled against religious and moral codes and artistic conventions.

The theatre as an institution underwent major changes during the latter half of the nineteenth century. The established theatres of Europe that had held state monopolies for centuries – such as the Comédie Française in France – were challenged by both popular commercial companies and the newly emerging experimental theatres. Strindberg's plays and theories were simultaneously inspired and embraced by the burgeoning independent theatres throughout Europe, a movement that started with André Antoine's fringe theatre, the Parisian Théâtre-Libre, in 1887. But even though, in the wake of Otto Brahm's production of *The Father* (1887) at the Freie Bühne in Berlin (1890) and Antoine's production of *Miss Julie* in Paris (1893), Strindberg became a sought-after playwright especially in Germany and France, his work still met with intolerance, lack of understanding, and outright censorship in Sweden. This compelled him to take charge of the production of his plays in several attempts (Copenhagen, 1888 and Stockholm, 1907) to create his own independent theatre company. Taking a distance from Sweden, which he felt was socially backward and repressive, also made it possible for him to become the first of the very few Swedish theatre artists to achieve an international reputation and gain a position at the forefront of the modern European canon. The chapters in this part discuss Strindberg's theatrical ventures, significant influences affecting his ideas on theatre, and the impact of his theatrical practices and theories.

Building on Strindberg's perception of life as performance, Part III ('Key plays') considers Strindberg's dramatic innovations and their contribution to the evolution of the modern theatre. In order to demonstrate how the playwright uses his life as the basis for experimentation with new dramatic techniques, this part samples plays from each phase and genre of Strindberg's dramatic writing. The plays of the 1880s testify to Strindberg's use of personal experience in dramatising the crisis of patriarchy and the dissolution of traditional masculine identities. Subsequent chapters lay out how the plays of the early 1900s constitute a new vision of the theatre, paving the way to major developments in the twentieth century. *To Damascus* part I (1898) and *A Dream Play* (1901), for example, represent a breakthrough in Strindberg's search for a dramatic form that corresponds with the experience of modernity, where life is divested of its substantiality and the subject is devoid of its coherence. The so-called Chamber Plays (1907–9) are the product of another experimental phase in which the experience of a changing culture is crystallised into plots constructed of abstract evocative patterns reminiscent of chamber music. The final chapter considers Strindberg's revision of the history drama genre, where Swedish kings, queens, and religious leaders are treated as modern characters entangled in both the domestic problems and the philosophical dilemmas of Strindberg's time.

Part IV ('Key plays/productions') explores the impact of Strindberg's work on the theatre culture of his time and beyond, including its relevance for our twenty-first-century theatre. The production and reception history of three of his most revolutionary contributions to the theatre – *Miss Julie* (1888), *A Dream Play* (1901), and *The Ghost Sonata* (1907) – are discussed, foregrounding how changing historical contexts shape the meanings of plays, enabling them to participate in contemporary cultural and political discourses through performance. The productions revisited include those at Strindberg's own Intimate Theatre in Stockholm (1907–9), interpretations by such historically significant directors as André Antoine and Max Reinhardt, and by international contemporary theatre artists, including Ingmar Bergman, Robert Lepage, and Katie Mitchell.

Strindberg perceived his time as one of fermentation and change. His incessant experimentation with drama and theatrical production was prompted by a desire to develop new forms that would correspond with his experience of dissolving beliefs, identities, and value-systems. In the 1880s he argued that the theatre of Europe was in crisis because artists and practitioners kept filling up the old forms with the contents of the new times, as a result of which 'the new wine has burst the old bottles' (Strindberg 1998: 56). Late in life he still warned the actors at his Intimate Theatre that 'no predetermined form is to limit the author, because the motif determines the form' (Strindberg 1966a: 19). This volume explores the contributions of an artist who felt compelled to continually respond to the shock of a culture in transition that ushered in European modernity.

PART I

Versions of a life

1 Problematics of biography vs autobiography

While there are a great number of Strindberg biographies and a massive body of Strindberg criticism incorporating a biographical approach to Strindberg's work, Strindberg 'the person' still remains an elusive figure and many factual details of his life are still disputed. There have been contradicting reports, for example, of the author's mental health throughout his life, the circumstances of his childhood, his relationship to his mother, and the ups and downs of his various marriages. Thus, for instance, symptoms of insanity described in Strindberg's autobiographical novels, *A Madman's Defence* (1887–88) and *Inferno* (1897), convinced several critics of the author's actual mental illness (see Brandell 1974: 66–97 and Jaspers 1977), while at least one biographer, Jan Myrdal, considers them as signs of normal, though most often repressed, reactions of an average person, and maintains that Strindberg exposes typical Swedish male attitudes and experiences still relevant at the end of the twentieth century (Myrdal 2000: 12–18, 72–82).

Another representative approach is that which demands adherence to factual truth from the autobiographical works. In his book exploring the author's psychological evolution as reflected in his writings, Torsten Eklund, for example, notes that facts of Strindberg's first marriage are clearly falsified in *A Madman's Defence* (Eklund 1948: 195). Some thirty years later Michael Meyer, who contends in his biography that Strindberg's autobiographies illustrate 'his unreliability as a witness' (Meyer 1985: 27), prefers to use his letters, diaries, and the testimonies of his contemporaries. But, as Meyer claims in his preface, 'Strindberg made enemies all his life' and therefore 'the evidence of enemies is as important to a biography as that of friends. Love can distort the truth as much as hostility' (Meyer 1985: xiii–xiv). Accordingly, he feels justified in citing the playwright's adversaries most extensively throughout his book. This method, however, fails to amount to a reliable or informative biography, and replicates instead the subjective and personal perspective that Meyer attributes to Strindberg's autobiographical writings.

Strindberg's apparent favouring of the autobiographical mode of writing gave rise to the 'biographical school' that has dominated Strindberg criticism ever since Erik Hedén's first Swedish biography, published in 1921, introduced the critical practice of reproducing the writer's life from his text and identifying the characters in his books with actual persons in his life. Subsequently Martin Lamm, the Swedish scholar who for the first time made use of a variety of external sources besides the texts, still proclaimed that 'by having depicted Strindberg's personality, one has already revealed the characteristics of his literary work. There are certainly few writers in world literature whose life and poetry are so completely united as his. ... To read him is the same as to live with him' (Lamm 1924: 19). But Lamm's reading of the work as life is highly misleading and problematic from a theoretical point of view, because it presents the purposeful composition of a literary text and the subjective workings of memory as unmediated truth.

A much more balanced perspective is offered by Swedish scholar Gunnar Brandell in his monumental four-volume biography, *Strindberg – Ett författarliv* (*Strindberg – The Life of an Author*), published between 1983 and 1989. In the preface to the first volume Brandell argues against critics who treat Strindberg's autobiography as fiction and discard it altogether as a valid source of information regarding his life. He considers the autobiographical works as memoirs that must be treated with caution because of the natural failings of memory and the distortions of stylistic devices that aim at shaping literary works out of life experience (Brandell 1983–89, vol. 1: 7). While Brandell considers the autobiography an indispensable resource in establishing Strindberg's perspective on himself at the time of writing the individual works, he richly documents his biography with what he calls 'external sources': diaries and letters of Strindberg's contemporaries, newspapers, and legal documents, including materials that were unavailable to Strindberg (Brandell 1983–89, vol. 1: 11–12).

The most helpful perspective is offered by Olof Lagercrantz's 1979 biography (translated into English in 1984), which assesses factual details recorded by Strindberg as 'rehearsals' and experiments for works to be written. He finds the autobiography 'useless as a source' because 'for every phase of his life, Strindberg decided how he wanted to be understood and deliberately created a persona for himself' (Lagercrantz 1984: 20). Reviewing Strindberg's correspondence in 1887 (the year in which *The Father*, the play in which the title character goes insane, was written), Lagercrantz notes that his letters became 'more bizarre than ever'. It is difficult to discern which elements of them are to be taken seriously and 'what is role-playing and sketches for creative work. It seems that he frequently appeared in the garb of his invented figures and spoke through their mouths' (Lagercrantz 1984: 170). Similarly, Lagercrantz regards the delusional quality of Strindberg's letters in 1896 as preparation for the autobiographical novel *Inferno* (1897):

> He recognized the entire region [Klam, Austria] as identical with the hell he read about in Swedenborg. The ravine resembled the entrance to the nether world in Dante. A pigsty by the road with its seven gates (which is still there) led his thoughts to the red-hot sarcophagi in the Canto X of Dante's *Inferno*. … Strindberg did not believe in it as a genuine identification: in his diary, he drew an entirely different building with six doors. … He arranged things, and was not a victim of delusions. He was looking for metaphors and symbols to use in his novel.
>
> (Lagercrantz 1984: 279)

Lagercrantz avoids collapsing the distinction between Strindberg's life and work; his concern is neither to credit nor discredit Strindberg's records of 'facts' occurring in his life, but to incorporate information as part of the creative process, allowing his readers insight into the intellectual and artistic crucible out of which the works emerged.

Critics' and readers' fascination with the author's personal life originates in Strindberg's own preoccupation with presenting his life in an extended series of autobiographical works. The best known of these are the four volumes – *The Maidservant's Son*, *Time of Ferment*, *In the Red Room* and *The Author* – written and published in 1886 under the comprehensive title, *The Maidservant's Son: The story of a soul's evolution*. But already the subtitle of the series suggests the arrangement of autobiographical material with a specific purpose in mind: to offer a Darwinian, evolutionist account of a life, in keeping with the naturalist quest to treat literature as a branch of progressive natural science. In 1904, long after he gave up naturalism, Strindberg sent a list of works to his German translator, Emil Schering, indicating that in case of his sudden death those writings should be included in a single volume of his autobiography with the title 'The Maidservant's Son'. The list comprised *The Maidservant's Son* (1886), *Time of Ferment* (1886), *In the Red Room* (1886), *The Author* (1886), *A Madman's Defence* (1887–88), *Inferno* (1897), *Legends* (1898), 'The Quarantine Master's Second Story' (*The Cloister*, 1898), *Alone* (1903), *The Occult Diary* (1896–1908), and his letters. 'This is the only monument I desire', he concludes the letter, 'a black wooden cross and my story' (Strindberg 1992: 712). What is striking about this list is the heterogeneity of genres designated as 'autobiography', including the author's diaries and correspondence. Moreover, the autobiographical mode extends to still other genres Strindberg worked in, including plays, novels, short stories, and essays, in all of which occur either direct references or veiled allusions to his own life events and experiences.

Thus, one of the most prevalent characteristics of Strindberg's writing is its self-referential nature, owing to his recurrent claim that an author's most appropriate subject is oneself, the single life that can be truthfully presented with the help of memory, whereas other people's lives remain to us a mystery. The preface to *The Maidservant's Son*, for example, consists of a mock interview with the author, who describes his book as 'the story of the evolution of a human being from 1849 to '67 in the middle of Sweden'

(Strindberg 1966b: 1), and then lays out his arguments validating the autobiographical authorial position:

> I think that the life of a single individual described at length and depth is truer and more enlightening than the life of a whole family. How can one know what's going on in someone else's mind? How can one know the complicated motives behind someone else's acts? How can one know what someone else said in an intimate moment? One can't. One fabricates, makes up. … There's only one person's life we really know and that one is our own.
>
> (Strindberg 1966b: 6)

This was written in 1886, during the heyday of nineteenth-century European naturalism, when Strindberg still subscribed to the idea that literature and theatre should break with fictional representations of life and people and strive for a scientific objectivity by gathering and presenting human data with as detailed exactitude as possible (Strindberg 1966b: 7–8). And even though by the 1890s he had become disillusioned with naturalism and searched for other means to reinvigorate drama and theatre, the autobiographical quest of projecting oneself into the work remained, but with a much different emphasis. From the late 1890s onward Strindberg grew increasingly suspicious of an observable, objective reality, and at the same time he was able to distance himself from his own life, past and present. His correspondence and plays of this period testify to his growing sense of the illusory and deceptive quality of the phenomenal world. Poet and writer characters in plays, such as *To Damascus* I and II (1898) and *A Dream Play* (1901), express their experience that poetry and dreams are more essential and authentic than the so-called external reality. The concept of the self as a volatile and temporary construction becomes an underlying theme in these plays in which characters seek in vain to reassemble fragments of their disintegrated identities. Thus the belief – reflected in the autobiographical works of the naturalistic period – that external reality (comprised of hereditary, social, and environmental factors) defines the self gave way to artistic techniques whereby notions of identity and reality are constantly tested, indicating a shift from a naturalist to a more radical and distinctly modernist aesthetics.

Youth and early work: 1849–72

It is, then, not an easy task to reconstruct a life that has so many variants and interpretations. In the following pages an outline of a basic factual background is provided to help discern the nature of myth-construction pursued by both the writer and his critics. Johan August was the first legitimate child of his parents, former servant girl and waitress Ulrika Eleonora Norling and the well-to-do shipping merchant Carl Oscar Strindberg. Ulrika Eleonora bore eleven children to Carl Oscar, of whom seven survived, before she died of tuberculosis in 1862. At the time of Johan August's birth, the Strindbergs lived in a spacious house by the so-called Riddarholm-port in central Stockholm bustling with lively commercial life, where Lake Mälaren meets the Baltic Sea.

The Maidservant's Son (1886) tells of Johan's (Strindberg's autobiographical self) first experiences of social injustice and class distinctions at an early age; as he observes how students from different backgrounds are treated differently at his first school in Stockholm – the Klara School for students of overwhelmingly wealthy background – and at Jacob's School for the lower classes, which he attended later. His empathy with the difficult lives of his destitute, lower-class peers, who often dropped out of school early and went on to work as sailors, reveals the perspective of the mature author/narrator looking back at his childhood and retrospectively constructing his image as 'the son of a servant woman'.

A more pronounced political outlook that took the form of social criticism started to take shape as Strindberg began his attendance at the University of Uppsala in 1867 and the following year took up elementary school teaching and tutoring in Stockholm. He was struck by the vast differences between the circumstances of his pupils in the poverty-stricken Stockholm slums and the privileged lives of the upper-class homes that could afford private tutoring for their children. All these experiences contributed to the rise of his political consciousness at a time when Stockholm was witnessing clashes between royalists and republicans, and the cultural impact of European social unrest, as evidenced by events such as the Franco-Prussian War (1870–71), followed by the Paris Commune (1871), contributed to increased tensions between the upper and lower classes of Sweden. As is apparent from several works depicting this period, such as *The Maidservant's Son* and the break-through novel *A Red Room* (1879), Strindberg sided with the oppressed and identified with the ideals of the French revolutionaries.

During the same time period Strindberg started preparations for medical studies by taking chemistry classes and apprenticing himself to the physician Dr Lamm, whose sons he tutored. As it turned out, however, he was more interested in becoming an actor and he took a job as a supernumerary at the state-funded Royal Dramatic Theatre in Stockholm in 1869. In the same year he completed his first play, which he tried to place at the Royal Dramatic Theatre, without success. Strindberg's earliest plays include *A Name Day Gift* (1869), a now lost two-act comedy about a conflict between a father and his son; *The Freethinker* (1869), about a teacher who loses his Christian faith; and the history play *Greece in Decline* (1869), later reworked as *Hermione* (1870). *In Rome* (1870), a comedy about Danish sculptor Bertil Thorvaldsen, was the first piece accepted and staged by the Royal Dramatic Theatre in Stockholm, and was received sympathetically (Lamm 1971: 16). His next play, *The Outlaw* (1871), a one-act piece set in twelfth-century Iceland, treating the conflict between paganism and Christianity, was also performed at the Royal Theatre and received bad reviews, but won the admiration of King Charles XV, who awarded the young playwright a small stipend (which, however, ceased upon the King's death in 1872, see Lagercrantz 1984: 33–34). This recognition encouraged Strindberg to leave his medical studies in Uppsala without completing a degree and he moved to Stockholm, where he supported himself as a freelance journalist, writing articles about social issues, critiquing the undemocratic educational system or the stifling power of Swedish bureaucracy for 'neo-liberal' papers (*Stockholms Aftonpost* and *Götebors Handelstidning*) (Brandell 1983–89, vol. 1: 120). He briefly worked as editor of the insurance magazine *Svenska Försäkringstidning*, only to be soon dismissed because of his sharp criticism of certain insurance companies and of the entire insurance business (Lagercrantz 1984: 46). Fleeing from his creditors in 1873, Strindberg travelled to the west coast of Sweden. After another unsuccessful attempt at becoming an actor in Gothenburg, he returned to the Stockholm Archipelago, an area he was deeply attached to until the end of his life. From the Isle of Sandhamn he wrote a series of sketches depicting the life of the people and the natural landscape in the Archipelago, which were published in the newspaper *Dagens Nyheter* (Lamm 1971: 41–47).

In 1872 Strindberg completed what is today considered not only his first masterpiece, but also the first modern Swedish drama (Brandell 1983–89, vol. 1: 129), *Master Olof*, a history play about Olaus Petri, the sixteenth-century leader of the Swedish Reformation. The play, which took nine years to move from page to stage, brought Strindberg a national reputation as an original as well as controversial playwright (see Part III).

The young writer and old Sweden: 1873–80

The span of Strindberg's lifetime was a politically and culturally turbulent era in Sweden. While the leading European countries had been undergoing modernisation and major social, political, and cultural shifts associated with scientific progress and the industrial revolution, Sweden's conservative monarchy and still nearly feudal estate system based on a rural economy lingered on. This conventional socio-economic organisation began to give way to a market economy, a bourgeoisie with more democratic leanings, and a labour movement, only towards the end of the nineteenth century. During the period of Strindberg's childhood and youth Sweden had four estates: the nobles, the clergy, and the burghers forming the upper class, and the fourth estate, which included the land-owning peasants and a miscellaneous group of soldiers, sailors, and both agricultural labourers and factory workers, constituting the lower class (see Strindberg 1966b: 11, n.1). The estate system remained in place until 1866, when the parliament, led by the upper class, which was dominated by the privileged nobility, was dissolved, opening the door for more democratic developments. While Brandell contends that Strindberg's early years coincided with the liberal reform period that eventually led to Sweden's complete transformation (Brandell 1983–89, vol. 1: 13), there was still a long way to go before a breakthrough could be achieved. Class privileges seemed to have been eliminated only nominally, and a plutocratic two-house parliament ruled the country, and in addition to the counts and barons now also included the powerful capitalists and bureaucrats. Women, and the majority of men, were still denied voting rights. It was as late as 1911 (a year before Strindberg's death) that voting rights for all men (including members of the former fourth estate) were introduced and the Social Democratic Party gained a presence in the parliament, balancing the power of the reactionary right-wing parties (see Scott 1988: 334–409).

From 1874 to 1881 Strindberg earned a living as assistant librarian at the Royal Library in Stockholm. In 1875 he met and fell in love with Swedish-Finnish Siri von Essen (1850–1912), whose family belonged to the Swedish minority in Finland – mostly members of the nobility – and who was at the time married to Baron Carl Gustaf Wrangel. Siri dreamt of becoming an actress, but because of her husband's high social standing as member of the Swedish military aristocracy she was not permitted to enter the profession. Only after her divorce from Wrangel was she able to make her debut at the Royal Dramatic Theatre. From the time of her marriage to Strindberg in 1877 she created on the stage several parts that he wrote for her, including the lead in plays such as *Sir Bengt's Wife* (1882), *The Stronger* (1888–89), and *Miss Julie* (1888).

In 1879 Strindberg wrote *The Red Room*, the novel that became an instant popular success. It is a bold and youthful piece of biting social satire and a realistic depiction of all strata of contemporary Stockholm society, from the working class, prostitutes, and Bohemians to the corrupt worlds of the Stockholm bureaucracy, insurance business and the press. Strindberg's deep attachment to his native city is made felt in the novel in a riveting, descriptive prose that combines lyricism with a concrete, realistic language, previously unprecedented in the Swedish novel.

Arvid Falk, the central character in *The Red Room*, is a young idealist who, in order to expose social injustices, chicanery, and profiteering, resigns from his privileged clerical post to become a journalist. 'The satirical sections', writes Strindberg to the Danish critic Edvard Brandes in 1880,

> are taken directly from life – at least in part. All the figures in the second chamber are taken from the Proceedings of the Riksdag [Parliament]! The account of the Triton business is partly reprinted from published accounts of the Neptune [a Swedish insurance company], which crashed, etc. That's why the enemies of light cried 'it's a lie!' for you see, it was all true!
> (Strindberg 1992: 77)

Characterising his political beliefs in the same letter to Brandes, Strindberg declares himself

> a socialist, a nihilist, a republican, anything that is opposed to the reactionaries! And from instinct, for I'm Jean Jacques' [Rousseau's] *intime* where a return to Nature is concerned: I'd like to join in turning everything upside down, in order to see what lies at the bottom; I believe we are now in such a state, so dreadfully regulated, that things can't be straightened out, it must all be burned down and blown up, so we can start afresh!
> (Strindberg 1992: 77)

In writing the novel Strindberg not only drew on his experiences as a journalist, but also used the unmediated, fresh language of a journalist with a sense of urgency that subverted the traditionally elevated and dignified Swedish novelistic style. By virtue of its bold treatment of politically dangerous contemporary themes and its style that thwarted generic expectations of an idealised representation of society, *The Red Room* ushered in modern Swedish literature.

Exile: 1881–83

But Strindberg enjoyed his triumph in Sweden for only a brief period. In 1881, when *Master Olof* was finally performed in Stockholm and gained a favourable reception, Strindberg gave up his job at the Royal Library to dedicate himself entirely to writing. He had grand plans, but also a sense of foreboding. While working on a volume of essays in 1881 he wrote again to his confidant, Edvard Brandes, 'When I've completed my cultural history, which will unmask the whole Swedish Nation, I shall go into exile in Geneva or Paris and become a real writer!' (Strindberg 1992: 82). This book became *The Swedish People at Work and Play, in War and Peace, at Home and Abroad, Or, One Thousand Years of the History of Swedish Education and Customs* (1882); a cultural history of Sweden from the perspective of the common people. It was both an ambitious and a politically highly provocative work, written in opposition to the official history writing and personally attacking the late Erik Gustaf Geijer, Sweden's foremost historian, who, as Strindberg wrote in *The Swedish People*, had regarded only 'the King's lackeys as members of the Swedish people' (Lagercrantz 1984: 97). This work was profoundly inspired by the British cultural historian Henry Thomas Buckle (1821–62), whose *History of Civilization in England* (published in Sweden in 1871–72) was designed as a 'different kind of history, not a saga of kings and with chronicles of battles … but a history that would bring to light the underlying factors that governed the development of civilization' (Sprinchorn 1982: 188). Buckle maintained that cultures and nations evolved causally, based on natural and not on moral or spiritual laws, and he argued that 'man is a product rather than the maker of his times' (Palmblad 1927: 26), which sharply opposed the old Romantic school of history writing that had professed an individualistic conception of history. Another important influence on Strindberg's thinking on cultural history at the time was British social scientist Herbert Spencer (1820–1903), exponent of a Darwinist evolutionary conception of history and originator of the term 'the survival of the fittest' (Sprinchorn 1982: 26). Strindberg's next book, a collection of satirical sketches entitled *The New State* (1882), criticised all the political institutions of the Swedish state, including the monarchy, the military, and the Swedish Academy (and also its reactionary permanent secretary, Carl David af Wirsén, an attack that would cost Strindberg the Nobel Prize for Literature).

These works were written at the time of a prolonged economic depression in Sweden during the 1870s and early 1880s, when workers' strikes became more and more frequent and an organised labour movement emerged. Strindberg himself felt that '*The Swedish People* ... was to have been a Cultural History but turned out a political tract' (Strindberg 1992: 53). His work was hailed by a young generation of political radicals (including Hjalmar Branting, a socialist politician and publicist, later leader of the Swedish Social Democratic Party, founded in 1889), but mainstream critics and the powers that be claimed that he defiled the sanctity of national history writing by representing the country's ruling classes as hypocrites and criminals (Lagercrantz 1984: 94–99). As Strindberg felt his freedom of speech threatened, he decided to leave Sweden (Strindberg 1992: 98). In 1883 he took his family to Paris and then to Switzerland in order to escape the hostile atmosphere in his homeland. At the same time marital strains commenced, as Strindberg's flight from Sweden forced Siri to give up her acting career, which had just begun, and follow her husband, dragging along their three children and a nursemaid, into a nomadic way of life, frequently moving from place to place and crossing borders back and forth between Switzerland, France, Germany, and Denmark. During this first period of Strindberg's self-imposed exile, his persecution in Sweden continued and reached its peak in the so-called *Married* trial in 1884.

The woman question: 1884–86

Married (*Giftas* I, 1884) is a collection of short stories focusing on the institution of marriage, relations between the sexes, and gender roles in contemporary society. It was Strindberg's first significant contribution to 'the woman question': the debate about women's rights and standing in society, which had become a prevalent theme in the European public discourse at around the middle of the nineteenth century. A number of complex economic, cultural, and political factors brought these issues to the fore, such as, for example, the industrial revolution which increasingly worsened the living and working conditions in cities where lower-class women and children toiled practically as slave labourers, whereas middle- and upper-class women were confined to the domestic sphere, having no rights, nor any meaningful outlet outside marriage.

Married is the first work by Strindberg where he explicitly deals with questions of gender and sexuality in a contemporary social and political context. At this stage, as *Married* reveals, Strindberg's views on the woman question were quite contradictory. In the preface he argues against Ibsen's *A Doll's House* (which had premiered in Christiania, Norway, in 1879), claiming that Nora's plight only concerns ten percent of the Scandinavian population: the upper-class or 'cultured woman' (Strindberg 1972: 30). With Rousseau, with whose writings he had been familiar since the 1870s (see Strindberg 1992: 37, 43, 77), he argues that in rural societies men and women are naturally equally based in their equal share of both work and goods. From the very outset he thus sets up the traditional nature–culture dichotomy in which women are excluded from culture and are reduced to their 'natural' role as mothers. A childless woman is neither a woman nor a man, he declares, but an unnatural hermaphrodite (Strindberg 1972: 31–44). In a second preface, however, Strindberg outlines his suggestions for 'Women's Rights' in a future society (Strindberg 1972: 44). Here he argues for equal opportunities in education and profession, voting rights (it was not until 1921 that universal voting rights for women were introduced in Sweden, see Scott 1988: 476–98), and access to the knowledge necessary to fill government positions. Women working outside the home, suggests Strindberg, would share their income with the family equally with men, but those who also work in the home should keep their salary to themselves, so that domestic work will not reduce them to slavery. Among several other suggestions, Strindberg includes the idea of separate rooms for each spouse, to ensure that women have control over their own bodies. In conclusion, he declares that women and men should fight together, as friends and not as enemies, to attain their freedom from crippling social confines (Strindberg 1972: 44–48).

The stories in *Married* explore various aspects of bourgeois marriage, morality, and sexuality. 'A Doll's House' tells the story of how an 'emancipated' spinster sets out to ruin a happy marriage by using Ibsen's play to enlighten the wife about the horrors of her married life. The story has a happy ending in that the marriage is saved and the spinster's ulterior motives are exposed. 'The Reward of Virtue', in which a naive young man falls victim to sexual double standards, features satirical discussions of masturbation and prostitution. It was this story that gave the Swedish authorities a reason to ban the book a week after its publication and call Strindberg to stand trial, charged with 'blasphemy against God or mockery of God's word or sacrament' (Strindberg 1972: 14). The passage that served as grounds for the lawsuit describes the Christian rite of confirmation as an 'agitating performance, at which the upper classes force the lower classes to swear by the body and word of Christ that they will never concern themselves with what the latter do', and mocks the Eucharist as an 'impudent deception practiced with Högstedt's Piccadon at 65 *öre* half gallon, and Lettström's wafers at 1 crown a pound, which the parson passed off as the body and blood of Jesus of Nazareth, the agitator who had been executed over 1800 years earlier' (Strindberg 1972: 71).

When, in 1884, Strindberg reluctantly returned to Sweden to stand trial, the event turned into a public controversy, used by political parties at either end of the spectrum to advance their agendas. The conservative right, including the Swedish Church and high-ranking members of the Court, campaigned with the assistance of the right-wing press to rid themselves of the notorious author for good. The left, including the liberal intellectuals and the young social democrats, celebrated Strindberg's acquittal as a victory for free speech. In reality, however, the trial and Strindberg's subsequent persecution made it impossible for him to make a living in Sweden as an author (see Brandell 1983–89, vol. 2: 62–63 and Strindberg 1972: 14–20). His demonisation continued even after he had fled back to Switzerland, and reached its climax in 1887 when John Personne, a respected educator and theologian (later bishop), published a pamphlet entitled *Strindbergian Literature and Immorality among Schoolchildren*. Strindberg's violent rejection by the Swedish cultural and political establishment affected his career and defined his image in Sweden, for many years to come, as the devil incarnate, a morally dangerous menace to society.

The *Married* trial became a watershed in Strindberg's personal, political, and creative life. In a sequel, *Married* II (1886), he lashed out at feminists who he believed had instigated the trial. This work marks a definite turn in Strindberg's outlook on women's liberation, to which he had been sympathetic in earlier years. The preface starts out with a series of quotes and paraphrases – by such authors as Schopenhauer, Aristotle, Rousseau, Darwin, Max Nordeau, Herbert Spencer, Annie Besant, and John Stuart Mill – that seem to provide scientific and philosophical proof of women's inferiority or society's negative discrimination of men (Strindberg 1972: 193–96; on the significance of these authors for Strindberg see ibid. 11–26). Following this introduction, Strindberg sets out his views on women's rights in complete opposition to those in the first volume, denouncing women as liars and tyrannical idlers incapable of any constructive contribution to society, who therefore should be denied the right to work, to vote, and to own or inherit property (Strindberg 1972: 197–207). But when one tries to match the dramatist's life with his politics, some puzzling contradictions emerge. In his personal life Strindberg preferred to associate with independent professional women, and all three of his marriages were, or at least started out as, mutually supportive creative partnerships. Yet, at the same time, in works such as *Married* II or *A Madman's Defence*, Strindberg glorified motherhood as women's only natural role, and represented men, including himself, as the victims of unnatural 'half-women': women who rejected motherhood as their sole vocation.

Critics, who attempted to understand these contradictions, offered various explanations. Harry Järv, who juxtaposes Strindberg's anti-establishment political thinking, his progressive views on some social issues – especially his empathy with the oppressed classes – and his conservative theories regarding the woman question, finds him a 'reactionary radical' with ever-shifting ideological commitments (Järv 1981: 78–86). Evert Sprinchorn contends that while, in comparison with Ibsen, Strindberg might appear a 'misogynist with a mother fixation' (1982: 218), it is because he created his own distinctive kind of literature by taking up the leading social questions of the time: feminism and the rise of the lower classes. On the former he took a stand on the right; on the latter, a stand far to the left. ... The woman question, which was debated even more intensely in Scandinavia in the 1880s than in America in the 1960s and 1970s, resolved itself in Strindberg's mind into class question, since all the feminists were from the upper classes ... in league with the moralists and monarchists.

(Sprinchorn 1982: 3–4)

Michael Meyer observes in his biography that '[i]t was not until he became disillusioned with marriage, and the sex war replaced social and political matters as his primary theme, that [Strindberg] became a major writer' (Meyer 1985: 114), implying that Strindberg could reach a wider, international audience only after switching focus by departing from uniquely Swedish political issues. But while Meyer states that it was the controversy around Strindberg's avowed misogyny that made him a much-debated figure in France rather than his plays (Meyer 1985: 312–15), Sprinchorn finds that 'French plays and novels written from 1860 to 1886 were more blatantly misogynistic than anything Strindberg had written, and he felt that his views on the woman question, if expressed in the fashionable mode of a play about a demonic woman, would be given a more sympathetic hearing in France than they received in Sweden' (Sprinchorn 1982: 46–47). Other readings point to the influence of contemporary intellectual currents, including Darwinian science and Nietzschean philosophy, that held on to the patriarchal status quo against the threatening figure of the independent 'new woman' (Fahlgren 1994b: 13–33, Robinson 1998: 194–207, Shideler 1999: 3–28). The theory of evolution provided 'scientific evidence' of male superiority and of women's natural role as mothers. Strindberg's views reflect the Victorian polarisation and marginalisation of the feminine in the images of the Madonna and the whore. Yet, as several critics agree, Strindberg the artist contradicts Strindberg the theorist when he creates strong female characters of striking complexity (Monié 1981: 21, Fahlgren 1994b: 124–26) in the so-called naturalistic plays such as *The Father* (1887) or *Miss Julie* (1888) and in the later dramas, including *Dance of Death* (1900), *Easter* (1900), or *Queen Christina* (1901).

Battle of the brains: 1887–90

The late 1880s was a period marked by the birth of a series of important works, including the so-called naturalistic plays – *Comrades* (1886–87), *The Father* (1887), *Miss Julie* (1888), *Creditors* (1888), *The Stronger* (1888–89), and *Pariah* (1889) – which brought Strindberg international fame with performances in the progressive independent theatres of Paris, Munich, and Berlin, while he was still anathema in Sweden. With these plays and other writings of the period Strindberg was keen on constructing his image as a leading naturalist playwright and theatre artist. In 1889 he and Siri created the short-lived Scandinavian Experimental Theatre in Copenhagen, modelled on André Antoine's Théâtre Libre in Paris, the renowned crucible of naturalist theatre (see Part II).

Following the lead of French novelist Émile Zola, the naturalists sought to create works of art that presented 'human data' by means of objective scientific methods such as observation, analysis, and experimentation. In his famous essay 'Naturalism in the Theatre' (Gerould 2000: 235–67), published in 1881, Zola urged dramatists to provide in their plays scientific analyses of their times and argued that the characters' actions should be determined by their environment rather than by abstract spiritual ideals. Consequently Zola attributed great significance to specific stage sets and costumes that would show the dramatis personae as products of their milieu. Based on evolutionary determinism, the naturalist aesthetics thus demanded that authors observe the role of heredity, the socio-economic milieu, and the given moment in their depiction of human behaviour (see Törnqvist and Jacobs 1988: 16–17).

As much as Strindberg was eager to follow this latest literary and theatrical trend, he was from the outset suspicious of the naturalist demand of a detached and unselective observation of life, and promoted what he called a 'greater naturalism'. In the essay 'On Modern Drama and Modern Theatre' (1890) he outlines his own brand of naturalism while criticising the French naturalist play-wright Henry Becque, whose play, *Les Corbeaux*,

> is photography which includes everything, even the speck of dust on the camera lens, ... this is the kind of misconceived Naturalism which believed that art simply consisted in copying a piece of nature in a natural way, but not the greater naturalism which seeks out those points where the great battles take place, which loves to see what one does not see every day, which delights in the struggle between natural forces, whether those forces are called love and hate, the spirit of revolt, or social instincts.
>
> (Strindberg 1996: 77–78)

In this text, then, as well as in his plays written between 1887 and 1890, Strindberg constructs his own 'greater naturalism' as a 'battle of the brains' (Strindberg 1996: 25–46), presenting fierce psychological struggles between characters for the survival of the fittest; a technique he found more dramatically effective, more interesting and truthful than putting on stage 'physiological' beings who were merely products of their material environment and heredity. Therefore, in terms of theatrical naturalism, Strindberg considered himself a leader, rather than a follower. He felt that both his plays of the period and his theories of the stage formulated in the preface of *Miss Julie* (see Part II) were revolutionary, compared to the dramatic experiments of the French naturalists, such as Zola and Becque.

Wanderer through Inferno: 1891–97

But in the 1890s Strindberg lost interest in naturalism and recast himself and his aesthetics once again in a new mould. Having divorced from Siri in 1891, he started a new life in Berlin where he was part of a circle of bohemian artists and writers, including Norwegian painter Edvard Munch and Polish author Stanislaw Przybyszewski, who regularly met at the tavern Strindberg christened 'To the Black Piglet' ('Zum schwarzen Ferkel'). It was here he met his second wife, Austrian journalist Frida Uhl, with whom he had a daughter, Kerstin, in 1894. This year also marked the commencement of the creative and psychological crisis Strindberg called his 'Inferno', which would last until 1897. Leaving his wife and newborn child behind in Austria, Strindberg settled in Paris, the capital of modern Europe, with grand plans for making his fame as a leading dramatist. During the crisis years, however, he gave up playwriting altogether and devoted himself to such diverse activities as painting and photography as well as studies and experiments in chemistry, alchemy, mysticism, and occultism, all the while publishing articles in French periodicals on subjects in these fields. His accounts of the period in the autobiographical novels *Inferno* (1897) and *Legends* (1898) depict bouts of acute mental suffering and a sense of constant persecution. During this period Strindberg showed no interest in the theatre. But when in 1898 he finally completed a new play, *To Damascus* part I, there was no trace of his previous naturalism (see Part III). It seemed as though his entire 'Inferno Crisis' (1894–97) were channelled into his reinventing himself as a dramatist.

Homecoming: 1898–1912

Having returned to Sweden in 1897 after many years abroad, Strindberg entered the most prolific period of his playwriting career. At the dawn of a new century he created works that became milestones of modern Western drama, including the *To Damascus* trilogy (parts I–II 1898, part III 1901), *Dance of Death* (parts I and II, 1900), *A Dream Play* (1901), the Chamber Plays entitled *Thunder in the Air*, *The Burned House*, *The Ghost Sonata*, *The Pelican* (1907), and *The Black Glove* (1908). He also completed a series of plays on Swedish history, including *Erik XIV* (1899), *Queen Christina* (1901), and *Charles XII* (1901). As earlier plays, including *The Father* or *Miss Julie*, the works following the Inferno Crisis dramatise unconscious mental processes and a sense of a fragmented, disintegrating self, but they depart entirely from realistic staging techniques. By the time Strindberg wrote the first part of *To Damascus* he had arrived at the conclusion that what we consider 'external reality' consists of 'only cerebral phenomena' (Strindberg 1996: 166).

Here Strindberg paraphrases from the German philosopher Arthur Schopenhauer's influential work, *The World as Will and Representation* (1819), which had a profound impact on his late drama, including *To Damascus* and *A Dream Play*. In order to render a sense of complete dissolution of an objective reality in these plays, Strindberg felt compelled to abandon the traditional manner of plot construction and characterisation. These plays operate with an introspective, associative logic rather than the traditional plot-based, cause-and-effect structure of the earlier period, and the characters' inner worlds – dreams, visions, hallucinations – are reflected in their environment and in the landscape.

After an initial sojourn in the southern Swedish town of Lund, Strindberg settled again in his native city, Stockholm, in 1899. Although by now several of his plays were staged here more frequently, *Miss Julie* still hadn't received its Stockholm premiere, which was finally to take place in 1906, sixteen years after it was written. *A Dream Play* was first produced in Sweden in 1907, six years following its completion. The Swedish theatre was still not ready to embrace a playwright like Strindberg, whose vision of the stage was so much ahead of his time. Besides ideological and moral concerns, his unconventional dramaturgy was met with confusion and the technical demands of his experimental plays also raised insurmountable difficulties for the theatre of his time.

In 1907 Strindberg's dream of an experimental theatre of his own finally came true when he and the young actor-manager August Falck (whose touring company had brought *Miss Julie* to Stockholm in 1906) opened the Intimate Theatre in Stockholm. In this theatre – the idea for which was inspired by Max Reinhardt's Kleines Theater and Kammerspiele in Berlin and by Georg Fuchs' Munich Art Theatre, among others – Strindberg was able to try out many of his ideas for the staging of his plays. Between 1907 and 1909 he interacted with the company on productions not only as a playwright but also giving directorial notes to actors and specific advice on design, acting style, diction, music, interpretation of lines, and much more (see Part II).

One of the most important influences on Strindberg's drama after the Inferno Crisis was the eighteenth-century Swedish visionary theologian, Emanuel Swedenborg (1688–1772). In his main works, including *Heaven and its Wonders and Hell* and *Arcana Coelestia*, he expanded his theory of correspondences, which profoundly informed Strindberg's so-called dream-play-technique. Swedenborg proposed that by reading and interpreting signs scattered throughout the physical world, one might catch glimpses of hidden spiritual dimensions. This inspired Strindberg to see everything with a double vision and to suggest – in both his plays and painting – an apparent ('exoteric') and a hidden ('esoteric') aspect of all things through visual analogies (see Sprinchorn 1982: 103–21, 264–66 for more on Swedenborg's influence on Strindberg).

Strindberg met his third wife, actress Harriet Bosse, some thirty years his junior, as he searched for a leading lady for the 1900 premiere of *To Damascus* part I at the Royal Dramatic Theatre in Stockholm. Subsequently, many of the new plays were inspired by or written for her, including the role of Agnes, the daughter of the Indic god Indra, in *A Dream Play*; the clairvoyant Eleonora in *Easter* (1900); and the title character in the fairy-tale play *Swanwhite* (1901), which was his wedding gift to Harriet. But the marriage was strained from the beginning, and Bosse left Strindberg temporarily when she was pregnant with their daughter Anne-Marie (born 1902). The couple permanently separated in 1903, but shared custody of Anne-Marie until Harriet re-married in 1908.

In his last creative period Strindberg combined religious mysticism with political radicalism. Upon his return to his homeland in 1897, he was criticised by the political left for his newly found religiosity and mysticism, and for having abandoned the quest for social justice he had so fervently pursued in his youth. But Strindberg never stopped forging new surprises. Yet another scandal arose in 1907 when he published the novel *Black Banners* (1904), a scathing satire on the conservative and corrupt literary establishment of the times. In 1910 he launched a press debate – known as 'The Strindberg Feud', which lasted for two years – on politics, religion, and literature, attacking the cultural elite and the poets of the old aristocracy. Taking up once again the fight for social justice in the cultural arena gained him back the support of the Swedish Social Democrats, the working class and students craving for change. This became apparent when, on his sixty-third birthday (22 January 1912), the 'people's poet' – who had been forced into exile thirty years before – was celebrated with a torchlight procession of some ten thousand students and workers passing under the balcony of his last apartment in Stockholm, which he had nicknamed the Blue Tower. In addition, a fund raised by national subscription (organised by the Social-Democratic leader Hjalmar Branting) was presented to him as the 'Anti-Nobel Prize', intended to compensate him for not being awarded the Nobel Prize in Literature (Lagercrantz 1984: 378). He died of stomach cancer on 14 May 1912. On his final journey a vast crowd of some fifteen thousand mourners (Persson 2004: 145), including the Social Democrat members of the Swedish parliament, and students' and workers' organisations under a forest of red banners (Persson 2004: 383), followed him all the way from his Blue Tower to the Stockholm Northern Cemetery, along the path that in his last play, *The Great Highway* (1909), serves as the background to the allegorical summation of the artist's passage through life.

2   Between fiction and reality

Madman and genius, Titan and barbarian, woman hater and the people's poet – these are just a few of the many labels often attached to August Strindberg's name. Strindberg's efforts to shape his own image were instrumental in that his controversial figure still looms above his work. Scraps of a life of which every aspect was made deliberately public in the name of literature or theatre and testimonies by acquaintances, fellow artists, and political, religious, scientific, and legislative authorities have provided inexhaustible source material for Strindberg criticism over the past century. An overview of Strindberg's reception, from his own time to today, reflects intriguing historical changes and topical variants in the public consciousness that have produced critical approaches and their apparatuses. The following pages attempt to contextualise some of these diverse accounts – by both Strindberg and his critics – and identify significant instances in his life that served as ground for myth construction.

Scapegoat and sacrifice

The fabrication of roles is a fundamental impulse underlying Strindberg's work and artistic evolution and therefore it is a crucial factor for the understanding of his theatre. Strindberg's tendency to identify with mythical figures and thus adopt various personae in his texts can be traced back to his childhood and adolescence, the years of his upbringing in Stockholm. At the time of his birth the family lived in a comfortable middle-class environment in an apartment house in Stockholm, from which they soon moved to a more spacious house in a pleasant suburb called Nortull. Even the bankruptcy of the family's steamship business in 1853 did not affect their growing prosperity. Yet, notwithstanding evidence to the contrary, *The Maidservant's Son* (1886) depicts 'Johan's' childhood as profoundly defined by the experience of hunger, cold, and destitution – emotional as well as physical. The first chapter is evocatively titled 'Afraid and Hungry'. The fact that, despite material comfort, Strindberg stresses an overwhelming sense of loss and abandonment as his earliest experience is often attributed to his mother's death of tuberculosis when August was thirteen. His distress was only aggravated by his father's second marriage, within a year, to the children's governess, thirty years his junior. Strindberg resented this union, and in *The Maidservant's Son* has his alter ego identify with both Hamlet and the biblical outcast Ishmael, revealing early on what Harry G. Carlson characterised as a profuse mythopoeic imagination (Carlson 1982: 7–35). Carlson notes that Strindberg's interest in myth and his utilisation of a rich texture of mythic references in all his works, including his autobiographies, had been long neglected by critics because of the conventional association of mythological thinking with pre-scientific primitivism and insanity. Carlson, on the other hand, regards Strindberg's interest in myth as a vital inspiration and source for his creativity (Carlson 1982: 3, 11).

A consistently recurring role throughout Strindberg's oeuvre is the author as a Christ-like figure, a scapegoat and a sacrifice, who, as one of Strindberg's many writer alter egos declares, in order to write his collected works, sacrificed his life, his person (Strindberg 1995: 147). The sacrifice theme reveals only one of those elements that make apparent the conscious re-shaping of lived experience via role-play in Strindberg's work. As already noted in the Overview, he fictionalised even the circumstances of his birth. In his biography Lagercrantz quotes a letter written to a friend in 1896, in which Strindberg states that he was born under the sign of the 'Ram', that is, Aries, which 'represents Sacrifice': to suffer only to be butchered in the end (Lagercrantz 1984: 13). Though Strindberg's actual birth date falls under the sign of Aquarius, the scapegoat/sacrifice role underlies the entire autobiographical writing and many of his plays. Brandell also points out a series of 'errors' already at the beginning of the first chapter of *The Maidservant's Son*, where Strindberg describes the circumstances of his birth:

> Three children had been born before [his parents'] marriage and John soon after. Probably he had been an unwanted child, as his father had gone bankrupt just before his birth, and the child first saw the light of day in a house that had been plundered and stripped bare except for a bed, a table, and a couple of chairs.
>
> (Strindberg 1966b: 15)

Brandell provides evidence to the contrary of Strindberg's assessment (that is, that Strindberg's father did not go bankrupt until years later and the family led a fairly affluent life; Brandell 1983–89, vol. 1: 12). But Brandell's claim that Strindberg's autobiography frequently falls short of the facts misses the point that the author's concern here is clearly to present himself as outcast and scapegoat. The Christ-like figure of the self-sacrificing martyr lives in Strindberg's work alongside the biblical Job, unable to comprehend his afflictions meted out by an unmerciful God (*Inferno*, 1897), and Jacob wrestling with the Angel (*Legends*, 1898). In what has been generally acknowledged as a 'confessional play', *To Damascus* I (1898), a hubristic Stranger, while passing the Stations of the Cross on his way to his symbolic Golgotha, challenges the gods, only to be ridiculed and humiliated by his alter egos, the madman Caesar and the haughty Beggar, and at the height of his agony chastised by a grim Confessor.

Constructing the writer

One of the chapters in *Time of Ferment* (1886), entitled 'He Becomes a Writer', relates how 'Johan' finds his calling as an author via a detour into the theatre world. He had long been attracted to a life in the theatre and fantasised about his acting debut in the role of the romantic hero Karl Moor in Schiller's play *The Robbers*.

He auditions as an actor at the Royal Dramatic Theatre in Stockholm, but is rejected. He feels so deeply humiliated that he decides to take his life with the help of an opium pellet, which he apparently keeps for that purpose. But since the opium fails to bring the desired relief of death, he goes out on a drinking binge in town. The following day, still in a delirious state, he experiences characters emerging from his memory, speaking lines and moving about as if on a stage. His first play appears in his mind as if completed by itself, and he simply records it on paper. Following this occasion, the narrator reports, 'the fever came on daily, and in two months he completed two comedies, a tragedy in verse, as well as a bunch of small poems' (Strindberg 1989: 261).

This story gives an interesting insight into how Strindberg shaped his own image through autobiography. Brandell cites evidence that Strindberg's story of his becoming a writer does not adhere to the facts of his life: his play *The Freethinker* was written already ten days before the failed audition (Brandell 1983–89, vol. 1: 95). Another interesting aspect of this story is the motif of attempted suicide, which recurs frequently in Strindberg's writing, including his fiction, plays, letters, and autobiography. If one reads these stories as factual accounts, they betray a mentally unbalanced person with suicidal tendencies. But Lagercrantz observes that 'apart from his own testimony there is no record of one suicide attempt' (Lagercrantz 1984: 31). Lagercrantz criticises Lamm and Hedén for taking the opium pellet seriously, and he reads Strindberg's frequent use of the suicide theme not as hard fact but as a symbol, through which he punctuates emotional high points in his life's story (Lagercrantz 1984: 32).

Indeed, if one considers the specific contexts within which Strindberg utilises the motif of suicide, it becomes clear that the stories are designed to create a strong dramatic effect on the reader or – when told by characters in a drama – on the listener. In *A Madman's Defence* (1887–88), the autobiographical novel that depicts Strindberg's first marriage, the young hero attempts suicide because of unrequited love by jumping into the ice-cold water on a boat trip, hoping he would die of pneumonia. While, after having successfully caught a cold, he stays in bed waiting for death, he still remembers to write a farewell letter to his beloved, who naturally rushes to the scene (along with her present husband) to take care of him. In the play *Miss Julie* (1888) the servant Jean tells his mistress how, as a young boy, he had fallen in love with her and in his despair attempted to take his life by lying down in an oat bin under an elder bush. On Jean's part, it is a highly successful device to win Julie's sympathy and ultimately seduce her (after which he tells her he had made up the whole story), but when, at the conclusion of the play, the idea of her suicide emerges as a solution to their situation, he suggests that she cut her throat with his razor; doubtless a much more effective method than taking an opium pellet or lying in an oat bin.

As far as the story in *Time of Ferment* about how Strindberg became a writer is concerned, it is clearly devised to have a strong effect on the reader, highlighting the event as a dramatic reversal that affects the entire subsequent life of Strindberg's autobiographical self. What is central to the story, then, is not its factual truth, but how Strindberg wants to be seen as a writer. In an effort to connect writing with acting, he depicts the process of writing as an ecstatic stage performance where role-characters emerge by themselves and are being enacted by the author as he transfers them onto paper. The opium pill and the subsequent drunken delirium help to create an effect of an initiation rite, a symbolic death and resurrection as a new person: the writer.

The maidservant's son

Just as importantly, Strindberg's autobiographical personae were constructed on the basis of his political views. As already the title of *The Maidservant's Son* suggests, he strove to be identified with his mother's lower-class heritage. The title hints at the biblical story of Ishmael, son of Abraham and the serving maid Hagar, who was driven out into the wilderness with his mother upon the birth of Abraham's legitimate son, Isaac (Gen. 16:12). Strindberg's mother, Ulrika Eleonora, was a tailor's daughter who was working as a waitress at a Stockholm inn when she met Carl Oscar Strindberg. Claiming his mother's humble background, Strindberg not only rejected his father on a personal and psychological level, but also aimed to override his actual bourgeois origins and inscribe himself on the Swedish political and literary map as a plebeian hero of the people.

Having lost battles against the conservative political and cultural establishment of Sweden in the early 1880s, he continued to culti-vate his image abroad as a radical free-thinker and anarchist. In an 1884 letter to friend Jonas Lie he depicts himself assassinating the Swedish king with dynamite (Strindberg 1992: 166). But as he felt usurped by both the political left and right of his country after the *Married* trial, he shed his plebeian identity and started experiment-ing with 'aristocratic radicalism' (Strindberg 1992: 294). He found inspiration in the philosophy of Nietzsche, whose works *Beyond Good and Evil* (1886) and *The Case of Wagner* (1888) he read in 1888. Strindberg now sympathised with the intellectual aristocrats who could rise above the confines of ordinary morality and com-passion for 'the weak' or, in his phrasing, 'the small' (Strindberg 1996: 6). In the novel *By the Open Sea* (1891), for example, he presents the story of an intellectual *Übermensch* (superman) who stands out in his environment and fails to find understanding among the common people. The central character is fishery inspector Axel Borg, who, upon arriving in a fishing village on a small island in the Stockholm Archipelago, sets about controlling and subjugating the native people and his prospective fiancée, as well as re-arranging nature through the power of his superior intellect. However, what betrays Strindberg's scepticism towards Nietzsche's ideas is that in the novel Borg fails in all of his attempts to establish his superiority, and instead he goes insane and perishes, abandoned by all, in the embrace of the indifferent open sea. Later, in *To Damascus* part I (1898), Strindberg criticises Nietzsche (and himself) in the figures of the supercilious Stranger and the madman Caesar. *A Dream Play* (1901) then takes a stand once again on the side of the suffering and the oppressed by presenting in vivid scenes the injustices and abuse that serving maids and coal-heavers are forced to endure; the public humiliation of the Lawyer who represents the needy; the 'sufferings' of the idle upper class caused by their over-consumption of goods and pleasures; or the petty political battles of the academic faculties, the supposed educators of youth. The revolutionary fervour of his youth, first apparent in *Master Olof* (1872), was then again resuscitated, even if mingled with a grain of mysticism, and social satire returned once more in *The Great Highway* (1909), Strindberg's last dramatic depiction of his time and his final self-portrait for the theatre.

Misogynist and madman

Characteristic of the late 1880s, in the aftermath of the *Married* trial in 1884 is the emergence of a new persistent and powerful combination of Strindberg-myths: that of the madman and the misogynist intertwined. Strindberg himself created this image through his works of the period, in which the rational order of patriarchy is typically threatened by contagious female irrationality and hysteria. Demonic women (such as Laura in *The Father*, 1887) or 'degenerated half-women' (Miss Julie), embodying the fears and fantasies of a male-dominated society, deliberately or unconsciously destroy their antagonist's reason (e.g. *The Father*). Personal records from the period seem to confirm that Strindberg indeed suffered from bouts of mental imbalance – just like the characters in his plays – in the late 1880s. Letters to friends and family members often reveal a fear of insanity, a bizarre obsession with his wife's assumed infidelity, and constant suspicion of being persecuted and spied upon (Strindberg 1992: 226, 233–36).

Lamm argues that the persecution mania Strindberg developed following the *Married* trial accounts for his violent attacks on women and feminists in the introduction of *Married* II (Lamm 1971: 157). But another reading of his life at this stage seems more helpful for the understanding of Strindberg's work and his creative process. The pathological obsessions in his personal letters are distinctly similar to those of the characters in his works. In this light, Strindberg's 'madness' seems to function as an assumed role – however convincingly enacted – that helps the author experience and express what he perceives as the evolving consciousness of the modern times, and helps him create experimental texts from the perspective of such experiences.

A profound interest in the psychiatric literature of his time is apparent from Strindberg's correspondence. In a letter from

Switzerland in 1886 to a Swedish author friend, Verner von Hei-
denstam, he writes that he owns 'a whole library on madness, from
which it transpires that everyone is crazy apart from the doctors'
(Strindberg 1992: 217). In his classic study entitled *The Battle of the
Brains* (*Hjärnornas kamp*, 1952) Swedish scholar Hans Lindström
traces Strindberg's readings of psychiatric literature (by such
famous, pre-Freudian physicians and psychiatrists as Hippolyte
Bernheim, Théodule Ribot, Jean-Martin Charcot, and Henry
Maudsley) and their specific impact on his writing in the 1880s. As
Strindberg's letters show, he prided himself on his knowledge of
the cutting-edge psychiatric research and exploited their findings in
his works in which he sought to present scientific 'case studies',
in accordance with naturalist principles. By calling his method
'vivisection' Strindberg meant to dissect his characters' souls in a
similar way to the physician who dissected bodies in order to
determine the cause of illness, and thus contribute to the scientific
understanding of his time. In 1887–88, for example, he wrote a
sequel to his autobiography in French, entitled *A Madman's
Defence* (*Le plaidoyer d'un fou*), which tells the story of his first
marriage from the perspective of the narrator/husband. As he
declares in the introduction, by writing this book he intends to
carry out experiments on his subject (his wife) in the mask of the
madman. The 'madman' of the title is then meant ironically, since
right at the outset the narrator is presented as a consciously and
coldly calculating rational mind.

The reception-history of this work is again twofold: on the one
hand, it indicates how Strindberg was successful in getting his
readers and critics to identify with the position of the fictional narrator, and on the other hand, it shows critics busy with firming
Strindberg's image as a madman and thus marginalising his voice in
the public discourse. However contradictory these two approaches
may seem, they are, in fact, interdependent. One typical example is
A. J. Uppwall's psychoanalytical study of Strindberg, in which
whilst analysing *A Madman's Defence* he declares,

> The Baroness [Strindberg's wife, Siri von Essen] embodied none
> of those traits which Strindberg admired in his mother, that is

the truly womanly qualities, but many of those qualities which he abhorred in his mother. This statement will be plain to anyone who will take the trouble to read [*A Madman's Defence*], which I have accepted as a fair and an essentially trustworthy characterization of the woman, even if somewhat overdrawn here and there, perhaps throughout.

(Uppwall 1920: 84–85)

Uppwall not only shares the narrator's sexist position, but also identifies the first-person narrator with the author and the female character with the author's wife, which results in a literary text turned into reality in the critical process. The work is treated as the discourse of an actual person lying on the analyst's couch. In his recent work Ulf Olsson traces how chiefly German and Swedish critics worked out Strindberg's psychopathology and identified him as a 'case', from the earliest contributions to as late as the 1990s. His 'madness' has been a means to place him in a marginalised group (that of the mentally ill), which was perceived as the Other, the same category to which women or criminals were relegated (Olsson 2002b).

During the years of his Inferno Crisis (1894–97) Strindberg increasingly contributed to the myth of his madness. The autobiographical novel (also written in French) *Inferno* (1897) gives a poetic account of the harrowing psychological and spiritual upheaval he suffered upon his arrival in 1894 in Paris, where, according to the narrator's testimony, he embarked on a hermit's life entirely devoted to science and alchemy. The novel conveys a pathological sense of being persecuted by former friends turned enemies, and of being punished and chastised by invisible spiritual powers. The work concludes with the rhetorical assurance that the narrator's (the implied author's) diaries from the period served as the basis of the book, which is a guarantee of its factual truthfulness.

More than any other work, *Inferno* has served as grounds for critics to declare its author suffering from schizophrenia, hysteria, paranoia, epilepsy, megalomania, persecution mania, narcissism, and much more (Olsson 2002a: 116–17, 130). In his study of the Inferno Crisis Gunnar Brandell, for example, establishes five consecutive psychotic episodes, based mainly on *Inferno*, *The Occult Diary* and Strindberg's letters from the period (Brandell 1974: 66–97). Karl Jaspers (1977, original German edition 1922) contributed with a comparative study of the psychopathology of Strindberg, Van Gogh, Hölderlin, and Swedenborg. And as late as 1992, Swedish psychiatrist Johan Cullberg concludes that Strindberg's portrayal of his creative crisis indicates serious psychotic episodes.

But if one seeks to understand Strindberg the artist rather than Strindberg the person, his 'madness' may actually help to discern what was going on creatively during the crisis years when he stopped writing drama and fiction, but in letters and in his *Occult Diary* (1897–1908) continued to record psychotic experiences, which were then systematically recycled in later works, including *Inferno*, *Legends*, and the *Damascus* trilogy. As discussed previously, Strindberg emerged from his Inferno Crisis with works cast in a new mould, leaving behind conventional dramatic techniques. Rather than the psychopathology of the characters and conflicts unfolding through the 'battle of brains', Strindberg's post-Inferno theatre dramatises the subtle internal stirrings of the mind and the workings of the unconscious. With this shift in focus, the themes of insanity and sexual warfare become less prominent. Thus, from the perspective of his post-Inferno dramatic writing, Strindberg's 'madness' seems to bridge the transition from the naturalism of the 1880s to the modernism of the 1890s and 1900s. Following the Inferno Crisis, then, Strindberg shed the naturalist and Darwinist scientific outlook that had previously shaped his art, but kept the insights he had learned from his psychiatric studies which, along with his newly found mysticism, helped him to develop new techniques for the staging of the modern self.

PART II

A life in the theatre

Strindberg's contributions to the theatre must be understood in light of his political attitudes and artistic stance, both of which positioned him for almost his entire career outside the domain of the theatrical establishment, while posthumously he was hailed as a pioneer of modernist theatre. His art was inspired by and, in its turn, nurtured the so-called independent theatre movement, which consisted of the numerous experimental companies that sprang up throughout Europe in the late nineteenth century (see Miller 1931 and Innes 1993). These companies offered alternatives to the theatre as a conservative institution maintaining the status quo. The first and most influential of these materialised in 1887 with the Théâtre-Libre in Paris, founded by the former gas clerk André Antoine, whose company functioned on the subscription basis, which helped to evade censorship and government control and opened the door to a modern repertoire and daring experiments in staging.

As an innovative dramatist, Strindberg challenged established staging practices with each new play. In the 1888 preface to *Miss Julie* he argued that the theatre of Europe needed a new mould for plays that would reflect the modern times. Some twenty years later he again sought to create a theatre that could accommodate his new plays reminiscent of chamber music. Since his experimental dramaturgy placed unprecedented demands on the stage, he set out to theorise and justify those demands, as we shall see in the following pages, in various important texts. When his dramas were accepted by mainstream theatres and producers ran into staging difficulties, he supplied cascades of practical suggestions that implied innovative new approaches to production, design, and acting alike. And since during his lifetime many of his plays were rejected by established theatres, Strindberg founded several experimental companies, with the intention of providing a venue for his own plays and creating a theatre of the future.

3 The Scandinavian Experimental Theatre

The first of these occasions occurred following the premiere of *The Father* at the Casino Theatre of Copenhagen in 1887. The production, directed by Hans Riber Hunderup, was given a highly controversial reception by the Danish press. While Hunderup and his future wife, Johanne Krum, were praised for their performance in the leading roles, most reviewers were shocked by the crude realism of the action and outraged by the sight of a straitjacket on the stage (Marker and Marker 2002: 6–7). Yet, encouraged by the relative success of the production, Strindberg was anxious to get two other recently written plays, *Miss Julie* and *Creditors*, produced in Denmark. He was soon disillusioned, as the commercial theatres kept rejecting them. He also had a number of new play ideas, but had no chance to get any of his work staged in his native Sweden. At the same time, Strindberg's wife, Siri, was desperate to return to her acting career. For these reasons the couple – with Siri as artistic director – founded the Scandinavian Experimental Theatre (Skandinavisk försöksteater) in Copenhagen, which after careful preparations opened to the public on 9 March 1889.

While the Strindbergs were still in the planning phases of creating their company in Denmark, where they lived at the time (see Chapter 1), there was a lively discussion in the Danish press about the theatre as an antiquated institution. As a consequence of the still-existing strict censorship and the monopolies held by the elite Danish Royal Theatre, many smaller companies had been struggling or gone bankrupt. These were circumstances that not only suppressed small commercial theatres but also hindered the appearance of a modern repertoire and new experiments in staging. Radical intellectuals, with the leadership of the well-known critic Edvard Brandes, argued for the abolition of censorship and the monopolies and for the benefits of a modern and more artistic theatre practice. Under these conditions many looked for a model to the Théâtre-Libre, which was exempt from censorship, since it functioned independently from both political authorities and the need of popular success for the company's survival. Each of its productions included several one-act plays and had a short run (no more than three nights, including dress rehearsals) for a select audience of subscribers who supported the cause of introducing new, international drama in contemporary settings and naturalistic staging, onto the French stage. The Libre's production style included individual *mise en scène* for each play, which would help to create the sense of an imaginary fourth wall through which audiences observed a 'slice of life', and suggested the deterministic force of the environment for the action and characters. Antoine also favoured natural and ensemble acting rather than star performances, and used box-sets and real stage properties – such as carcasses of beef to create a sense of a butcher shop – rather than painted scenery. Instead of footlights he used light sources that were justified by the plot, such as lanterns, relevant to the action (Knapp 1988: 17–61).

Strindberg closely followed developments at the Théâtre-Libre and was impressed by its goals from its inception. In his essay 'On Modern Drama and Modern Theatre' (1889) he subscribes to Antoine's practice of performing several experimental and contemporary short pieces (the '*quart d'heure*', a play that lasts a quarter of an hour) in an evening's bill (Strindberg 1996: 84–85). He immediately recognised the potential of a 'free theatre' and, shortly after the opening of the Théâtre-Libre, he made plans for creating a small travelling repertory company with Swedish actor and director August Lindberg (Törnqvist and Jacobs 1988: 33). Though Lindberg declined, Strindberg went on to elaborate plans for an experimental theatre of his own and on 17 November 1887 he posted an announcement in the Danish newspaper *Politiken*:

Since I intend as soon as possible to open a Scandinavian Experimental Theatre patterned after the *Théâtre Libre* in Paris, I wish to announce that I shall consider play scripts of all sorts, but I am particularly interested in relatively short pieces with contemporary settings, not requiring extensive machinery or large casts.

(Törnqvist and Jacobs 1988: 33)

Though Strindberg read many submissions, he was unimpressed by the majority of them and the company ended up including solely his work in its opening programme. While he avowedly intended to follow in Antoine's footsteps, he neglected the most important organisational component that helped the Théâtre-Libre not only to survive but also to revolutionise production practice and repertoire, allowing it to avoid censorship. By supporting itself solely from subscriptions by a select circle of audience members, the Libre placed itself outside the domain of public performances and thus it could work independently from the powers that be.

Strindberg looked to Antoine's theatre for an artistic model, but paid no attention to the structural model, and therefore the Scandinavian Experimental Theatre was vulnerable to both censorship and financial failure. The company was preparing for the premiere at the locales of the Dagmar Theatre in Copenhagen, with a programme that included three one-act plays by Strindberg: *Miss Julie* (1888), *Creditors* (1888), and *The Stronger* (1888–89). The Dagmar's censor, however, rejected *Miss Julie* on the grounds of indecency that had scandalised the public already upon its publication, even though many of the swear-words considered shocking had been cut from the dialogue (Ollén 1961:134–35). Undaunted, the company continued rehearsals with its programme unchanged, but in the middle of the dress rehearsal a notice of ban on *Miss Julie* arrived from the Danish Ministry of Justice, threatening to summon the police force if the company failed to comply. In despair, the short play *Pariah* (1889) was substituted for *Miss Julie*, and after a few hasty rehearsals the premiere at the Dagmar took place only a week later than planned.

Besides the organisational deviation from the Théâtre-Libre there were also major differences in production style. For the staging of his plays Strindberg supplied his own theories, closely related to his style of playwriting in this period, including a sharp focus on the characters' psychological struggles. As opposed to Antoine's staging practices, the set at the Scandinavian Experimental Theatre was utterly simple; reduced to a few pieces of furniture signalling a café or a seaside-resort; partly because of limited resources and partly because the external environment was not a major determining factor in Strindberg's plays. In a letter to Siri concerning the role of Mrs X in *The Stronger*, for example, Strindberg asked her to play the character as 'an actress, not an ordinary housewife' (Strindberg 1992: 307), thereby stressing the abstract, metatheatrical qualities rather than the realistic ones. Each of the plays performed (including the banned *Miss Julie*, which was eventually given two evenings of private performance at the Student Union of the University of Copenhagen) was written with the principles of a 'greater naturalism' in mind (Strindberg 1996: 78), and focused on the psychological struggle between the central characters. Consequently, the setting – which was the cornerstone of Antoine's naturalistic staging – played no major role in Strindberg's productions at this stage of his career.

A convincing presentation of psychological strife, however, would have required experienced performers. The Scandinavian Experimental Theatre included only one actor with considerable reputation, Hans Riber Hunderup, the former director of the Casino Theatre, playing the ex-husband Gustaf in *Creditors* and one of the two roles in *Pariah*. Critics generally praised him in both plays; as one audience member later commented, he was able to appear 'Strindbergian' thanks to his 'physical brutality'.[1] The young author Gustav Wied who played opposite him in *Creditors*, however, was ridiculed because of his amateurish performance. Along with Wied, whose speeches were inaudible, Nathalie Larssen (later to become a well-known Danish playwright), playing Tekla in the same play, was blamed by reviewers for the failure of the otherwise powerful triangle-drama. The performance of *Pariah* received most praise, with the young but relatively more experienced actor, Viggo Schiwe, playing opposite Hunderup. In *The Stronger* Siri Strindberg, who had been away from the stage for many years, was praised for playing the speaking role of Mrs X with dignity (Ollén 1961: 168–70, 175–77). But as a result of such a complex set of circumstances – including the ban, and organisational and artistic inconsistencies – the Scandinavian Experimental Theatre disbanded after only two performances of its initial production: one on the opening night at the Dagmar Theatre in Copenhagen and the other one week later in the southern Swedish town of Malmö.

There were two performances of *Miss Julie* in the small, run-down auditorium, with makeshift stage, of the Student Union in Copenhagen, where Siri von Essen Strindberg played Julie opposite Schiwe's Jean and Henriette Pio's Christine. Though Siri's performance was considered by critics to be weak and unconvincing, the piece scored a favourable reception, as critics noted the elemental force of the play that grasped the audience in spite of the shabby locale (Ollén 1961: 135–36). The brief history of the Scandinavian Experimental Theatre, however, ended with this performance, on a note of financial and emotional bankruptcy for the Strindbergs. Unable to survive long enough to make a mark, this theatrical venture nonetheless had great significance in helping Strindberg to establish himself as a household name within the independent theatre movement throughout Europe. All the surrounding controversies made the effort a highly publicised one and gained the support of progressive Scandinavian intellectuals – including the brothers Edvard and Georg Brandes – with continental reputations and connections. From the 1890s onward many of Strindberg's plays were produced by independent theatre companies (chiefly in France and Germany) before they reached the Swedish stage or the mainstream European theatres.

Note

1 Julius Clausen, 'Strindbergsteatern i Köpenhamn, som spelade en enda kväll', *Svenska Dagbladet*, 10 October 1921 (reprint of article from 9 March 1888).

4   Strindberg and the Independent Theatre Movement

The first productions

At the time of the Scandinavian Experimental Theatre Strindberg was still unwelcome on the Swedish stage (see Chapter 1). Although *The Father* (1887) received its Swedish premiere at the Nya Teatern in Stockholm in 1888, it was not until 1908 that the play achieved a breakthrough, with seventy-seven performances at Strindberg's next theatrical enterprise, the Intimate Theatre (Strindberg 1966a: 12). *Miss Julie* (1888) was not only banned from public performance in Denmark, it was also barred from the professional stage in Sweden for eighteen years after its completion. In 1890, however, *The Father* premiered at the Freie Bühne, another influential independent company, founded in Berlin in 1889 by the critic Otto Brahm. The Freie Bühne introduced naturalist drama and production style to Germany by staging the early works of Gerhart Hauptmann and popularising Ibsen and Strindberg. As opposed to Antoine, who worked with amateur performers whom he trained in the naturalistic acting style of his own devising, Brahm engaged professional actors, giving performances on Sundays when the professional theatres were dark. Thus, the title role of *The Father* was played by Emanuel Reicher, an admired star credited with introducing modern German acting, opposite Rosa Berten's Laura. This production was Strindberg's debut outside Scandinavia and his introduction to the German-speaking theatre, in which his work came to affect major modern developments. The German premiere of *The Father* at the Freie Bühne was soon followed by several significant productions of Strindberg's other naturalistic plays. *Miss Julie* was performed on a single night (3 April) in 1892 by Brahm's experimental company, with Rosa Berten in the title role and Rudolf Rittner as Jean, but because of the heated protests, especially by female audience members, no further performances were attempted. Emanuel Reicher played the Captain in *The Father* again at the Carltheater in Vienna in 1900, and initiated numerous Hamburg productions. *Creditors* (1888) was produced at the Residenzteater in Berlin in 1893 with some of the most prominent German actors of the time: Rosa Berten, Rudolf Rittner, and Josef Jarno. In 1899 Jarno was appointed director of the Theater in der Josefstadt in Vienna, where he produced *Creditors* in his first season, and became an avid promoter of Strindberg in Austria (Ollén 1961: 120, 139, 166). By the time the young Max Reinhardt opened his avant-garde cabaret, the Schall und Rauch in Berlin in 1901, there was a strong Strindberg tradition established in the German-speaking independent theatre. In his Kleines Theater (the successor to Schall und Rauch) Reinhardt produced a series of Strindberg plays, including *The Bond* (1892) and *Crimes and Crimes* (1899) in 1902 and the still-scandalous *Miss Julie* in 1904. Here Julie was played by Gertrud Eysoldt, who later became famous for her talent in presenting 'degenerated, boldly sensual, intellectually gifted women', and who achieved great success for several years with her performance as Strindberg's heroine (Ollén 1961: 138). These initial and sometimes controversial performances by independent companies during Strindberg's lifetime made him so popular in Germany that in the three years following his death – from 1913 to 1915 – 'there were more than 1,000 performances of twenty-four of his plays in sixty-two cities' (Innes 1993: 39).

In France it was Antoine's decision in 1893 to stage *Miss Julie* at the Théâtre-Libre in Paris that led to Strindberg's breakthrough as a key influence on the modern European stage. Pleased with the success of the performance, Antoine felt that 'Arquillière was extraordinary as the lackey' opposite Mlle Nau's Miss Julie (Antoine 1964: 217). *Miss Julie* was included in a triple bill with *The Brazilian Household* by Romain Coolus and *Down with Progress* by Edmond de Goncourt. '*Miss Julie* made an enormous sensation,' Antoine recorded in his diary on 15 January 1893. 'Everything stimulated the audience – the subject, the setting, the packing into a single act an hour and a half in length enough action to sustain a full-length French play. Of course, there were sneers and protests, but it was, after all, something quite new' (Antoine 1964: 216). The powerful effect of the performance was enhanced by the distribution of Strindberg's preface to the audience, which Antoine made sure to have translated and printed, for, as he noted a few days before opening night,

> Strindberg has written a rather lengthy preface, full of interesting things. ... He includes stimulating suggestions about raking the setting, suppressing the footlights, and lighting form above – clearly showing the German influence that I have long since welcomed from abroad.
>
> (Antoine 1964: 216)

The gloomy scenarios and shocking social and psychological revelations of contemporary Scandinavian playwrights such as Ibsen, Strindberg, and Bjørnstjerne Bjørnson were much in vogue in the Paris of the 1890s, and were frequently staged by companies with vastly different aesthetics. Conservative critics such as Francisque Sarcey, on the other hand, held that these dramatists were alien to the French stage, which had a much different tradition of its own, where lucid dialogue, classical play structure, and formal delivery were valued the highest (Antoine 1964: 217). But the growing modernisation of the French stage, thanks to the contributions of the independent companies, could no longer be hindered. While Antoine was the first to introduce a modern international repertory in France, the Scandinavian playwrights became a cornerstone in the programme of the symbolist Théâtre de l'Oeuvre, founded in 1893 by actor-director Aurélian-Marie Lugné-Poë, a former member of Antoine's troupe. As opposed to the naturalists, who were interested in putting the characters' external environment on stage, the symbolists turned to spirituality and dreams, attempting to render the inner life of the soul through the poetic atmosphere created by stylised painterly sets, dream-like incantation, and ceremonial acting style (Schumacher 1996: 87–96 and Knapp 1988: 69–153).

Thus, Strindberg's next Paris conquest took place in 1894, when Lugné-Poë mounted *Creditors* as part of the closing programme of the Théâtre de l'Oeuvre's first season. In the triple bill that included a one-act play by Danish writer-director Herman Bang and a dramatic poem by Henri de Régnier, it was again Strindberg's play that gained favour with both critics and spectators. *Creditors* (1888), originally written for the Scandinavian Experimental Theatre, was conceived as a naturalistic play with a focus on psychological warfare and 'soul murder' (Strindberg 1996: 23–63). Most likely it was the focus on the unconscious workings of the mind and the use of suggestion and thought transference as plot devices that made the play attractive to the symbolists. The staging, however, did not strictly follow the symbolist style. Like several other Scandinavian productions at the Théâtre de l'Oeuvre, *Creditors* was directed by the Danish Herman Bang, because of his appropriate cultural background. Bang, however, preferred focusing on the actors' work in the style of psychological realism and resisted Lugné-Poë's notion of elevated, poetic staging (Deak 1993: 210).

Strindberg had qualms about Bang's involvement, since the latter had previously declined to participate in the Scandinavian Experimental Theatre's production of the play in Copenhagen. To Strindberg's dismay, considerable cuts were made in the play, which he felt he had written with utmost economy. In this triangle drama Lugné-Poë played Adolf opposite Philippe Rameau's Gustaf and Lucienne Dorcy's Tekla – the latter two were guest artists, both from the Odeon theatre. Critics praised the acting and were fascinated by the psychological qualities of the characters (Deak 1993: 210–11).

There is more information preserved on the *mise en scène* of *The Father*, the very play that Strindberg had claimed to be strictly following the naturalistic formula (see Chapter 7), in the Oeuvre's second season in 1894. Again, Strindberg reluctantly allowed Henri Bauër, who had made the French adaptation, to cut several important passages from the text (Kvam 1991: 58). This production, also directed by Bang, used the theatre's 'Scandinavian set', familiar to spectators from productions of plays by Nordic dramatists. It consisted of a wallpapered room with a big stove next to a clock and a table with chairs and a lamp. A cloakroom could be seen upstage, where 'instead of military coats (as demanded by Strindberg) huge fur coats were hanging' (Kvam 1991: 58). In this simple but realistic set, Bang concentrated again on the psychological drama and emphasised emotional highpoints, which seems to have fascinated the audience. Such a riveting moment occurred, for example, when the Captain (Philippe Garnier) delivered his lines weeping and crawling at his wife's feet. Fearing that the Parisian public would find the protagonist's death following his confinement in a strait-jacket comic rather than tragic, the director also had the ending changed so that the Captain only suffered a nervous breakdown and was led away from the scene (Ollén 1961: 122).

In this production again, the actors came from different Parisian companies with varied backgrounds. Philippe Garnier was a melo-drama actor from the Porte Saint-Martin; Lucienne Dorcy (Laura), from the Odeon, had a more formal, classical stance; Louise France as the Nurse, from the Théâtre-Libre, was trained in the natural style; and Lugné-Poë, with his fondness for the hieratic manner, came on board in the role of the Pastor. Yet, this eclectic ensemble seems to have made a great impression on critics, who considered *The Father* the Oeuvre's most successful and exciting production to date (Ollén 1961: 122), and even Maurice Maeterlinck, the arch-symbolist dramatist discovered by the Oeuvre, praised Lugné-Poë's choice to put on this 'very beautiful play' (Deak 1993: 213).

5   Strindberg and stagecraft
Theory and practice

In an 1887 letter to French author Émile Zola, who was a devoted supporter of the Théâtre-Libre and the first theorist of theatrical naturalism, Strindberg described *The Father* as 'a drama composed with a view to the experimental formula, aiming to show the effect of the inward action at the expense of theatrical tricks, to reduce décor to a minimum, and to preserve the unity of time as far as possible' (Strindberg 1992: 243).

But Zola had some reservations about this approach. He demanded a comprehensive representation of life on stage where 'characters have a complete social identity' so that 'one can rub shoulders with them [and] they breathe the same air as we do' (Schumacher 1996: 303). Yet, it is Strindberg's preface to *Miss Julie* (1888) that still today is considered a practicable manifesto of the naturalist theatre, rather than Zola's more literary theories. Strindberg here derives all the elements of stage production from the demands of the modern age, including character, dialogue, play structure, set, lighting, acting style, and make-up. He insists that in order for the theatre to revive from its moribund state, it must present modern characters 'living in an age of transition more urgently hysterical … than the one that preceded it' and therefore 'more split and vacillating, a mixture of the old and the new'. Rather than artificially imposing fixed character traits, playwrights should create 'souls' that are 'conglomerates of past and present stages of culture, bits out of books and newspapers, scraps of humanity, torn shreds of once fine clothing now turned rags, exactly as the human soul is patched together' (Strindberg 1998: 59–60). Such characters become believable on stage only if their speech sounds naturally flowing and randomly wandering, 'presenting material in the opening scenes that is later taken up, reworked, repeated, expanded, and developed, like the theme in a musical composition.' The dialogue therefore must avoid the symmetrical, mathematical composition of French drama 'and let the characters' minds function irregularly, as they do in a real-life conversation, where no topic of discussion is exhausted entirely and one mind by chance finds a cog in another mind in which to engage' (Strindberg 1998: 71).

Since modern audiences have a diminished capacity to accept illusion, argues Strindberg, plays should be reduced to a single act so that they present the fluidity of life without the disruption of scene changes and intermissions. Three-dimensional sets must replace the traditional painted backdrops, and the actors should be able to move around freely in their natural environment. In order to achieve subtlety in the actors' facial expressions Strindberg calls for the reduction of make-up and the replacement of footlights with sidelights, for in a 'modern psychological drama ... the subtlest movements of the soul must be revealed more through the face than through gesture and sound' (Strindberg 1998: 75). He also wishes to see crucial scenes staged on the part of the stage where it is appropriate to the action rather than next to the prompter's box 'like duets intended to evoke applause' (Strindberg 1998: 74). These passages of the preface critique accepted practices of the theatre of Strindberg's time, especially the formal-classical and melodramatic styles favoured by nineteenth-century European producers and audiences. Against this background, Strindberg declares, he is content to initiate small modifications that would eventually lead to the transformation of the stage into 'a room where the fourth wall is removed' (Strindberg 1998: 74–75). In *Miss Julie*, Strindberg discloses in the preface, he experimented with a number of specific innovations, including complex character motivation, erratically shifting dialogue, and brief sections of monologue, ballet, and pantomime to ease the tension of the uninterrupted action. As for the scenery, he borrowed from impressionist painting the device of making a setting appear cut off and asymmetrical, thus strengthening the illusion. When we see only part of a room and a portion of the furniture, we are left to conjecture, that is to say, our imagination goes to work and complements what is seen. ... I have placed the upstage wall and the table diagonally so that the actors can play facing the audience or in half-profile when they sit opposite each other at the table.

(Strindberg 1998: 73–74)

Many of the practical suggestions Strindberg included in his preface to *Miss Julie* were far from being original, yet, it is the first and perhaps only systematic theory by a theatre practitioner for the modern naturalist stage, written just a year after the opening of the Théâtre-Libre. According to S. M. Waxman, chronicler of the Libre, Antoine went to the expense of translating and distributing Strindberg's preface to the audience because it gave him 'great many suggestions for his outline for a new playhouse. It was another step forward toward the twentieth century "little" theatre that has become almost universal' (Waxman 1964: 180).

While *Miss Julie* made its mark on naturalistic staging practices and on the independent theatre movement, Strindberg's post-Inferno plays had a great impact on developing modernist as well as post-modern staging techniques (see Part IV). Plays such as *To Damascus*, parts I and II (1898), *Dance of Death* (1900), *A Dream Play* (1901), and *The Ghost Sonata* (1907) were a result of a constant search for new forms and adequate production styles. By the time he returned to the theatre following the Inferno Crisis (see Part I), Strindberg's ideas on staging had also transformed and, following the latest developments in technology and design, he now envisioned stylised, non-realistic staging for his new drama. He sought to find ways in which episodic plays that evolve associatively at varied locations, such as the *To Damascus* trilogy and *A Dream Play*, could be performed without constant scene changes, cluttered realistic sets or romanticising scene painting. He felt his new work called for a dream-like, poetic effect of 'dematerialization' on stage (Strindberg 1966a: 289–93). Innovations on the independent stages of Europe continued to hold his keen interest and he became preoccupied with anti-illusionistic experiments in scenography and lighting. Thus, for example, he actively participated in the staging of his *To Damascus* I, which premiered at the Royal Dramatic Theatre in Stockholm in 1900. He urged director Emil Grandinson to create a simplified and stylised set that could suggest the nightmarish quality of the essentially internal action. In an interview published on the occasion of his fiftieth birthday, on 21 January 1899, in the Swedish newspaper *Svenska Dagbladet*, he envisioned an ideal stage for the play, outlining a theatre radically different from what he had advocated in the 1880s. As in the preface to *Miss Julie*, he still called for the elimination of heavy stage machinery, but the demand for realistic ambience had given way to an utterly simplified design that would indicate locations with the help of painted backcloths or by using evocative, non-realistic projections:

> I don't want to use ordinary theatre decorations for my new plays. All these old-fashioned painted theatrical rags must go! I only want a painted background representing a room, a forest or whatever it may be, or perhaps a background could be produced by a shadow picture painted on glass and projected on to a white sheet.
>
> (Bergman 1967: 15–16)

One of Strindberg's most radical suggestions was to replace the scenery entirely with slide projections on transparent screens in order to produce an effect of dream-like fluidity and 'dematerialization' (Bergman 1967: 36). As early as 1889 he had planned to create a fairy-tale play comprised of world-historical episodes, such as scenes from the French Revolution, projected by a large magic lantern (Bergman 1967: 16). His experiments with non-realistic stage effects, especially with projections, were inspired by such novel visual media of his time as the magic lantern shows and moving panoramas which were highly popular forms of entertainment in late nineteenth-century Europe (Hockenjos 2001: 169–82), as well as by his own experiments with photography and photogram in the 1880s and 1890s (Szalczer 2001: 42–52). The shadow plays that he had seen in the 1890s at the famous Paris cabaret, the Chat Noir, were another source of inspiration. Cabaret, a pro-liferating performance genre throughout *fin-de-siècle* Europe, pro-vided a suitable environment for avant-garde artists to casually experiment with new ideas and forms. Audiences at the Chat Noir, for instance, were fascinated by Henri Rivière's *Théâtre des Ombres* (Shadow Theatre), which featured zinc silhouettes of figures and landscapes placed and moved against a screen within a wooden framework. The screen was lit, through a series of coloured glass panels, by an oxy-hydrogen flame at the back of the structure (Cate and Shaw 1996: 58). Strindberg's enthusiasm as he watched these performances was so great that in 1894 he made plans to 'found a Chat Noir' where he would play the guitar, 'paint the walls and put on *The Keys of Heaven* as a shadow-play' (Strindberg 1992: 516).

For the production of *To Damascus* in 1900, then, Strindberg suggested that the scenery should consist entirely of projected background images. But after extensive experiments with magic lantern projections the idea had to be abandoned because of the poor technology available in Sweden at the time. The projected images became clear enough only when the foreground was dar-kened, which in turn undermined the visibility of the performers (Strindberg 1966a: 293).

But there were other experiments in the contemporary theatre that proved to be informative for Strindberg's post-Inferno ideas and practice of staging. In modern attempts that sought to recon-struct medieval and Elizabethan staging conventions he saw possi-bilities for simplification and a fluidity of performance that could be applied to the production of his multi-locale episodic plays. In his *Open Letters to the Intimate Theatre* he remarks how the perfor-mance of the seventeenth-century passion play originating in Ober-ammergau, Bavaria, and the so-called Shakespeare Stage in Munich 'helped bring simplified staging into being' (Strindberg 1966a: 290). The Oberammergau Passion Play, which had been traditionally staged once a decade, was widely publicised preceding its 1900 per-formance. It took place in a basilica-like structure – still functioning today – where the auditorium, covered with six giant arches, had a view of the open-air stage on which a set indicating various locales simultaneously was mounted (see Short 1910 and Huber and Stückl 2000). Strindberg also studied Jocza Savits's book on the Shakespeare Stage in Munich. This reform stage, which had been initiated by Karl von Perfall, Karl Lautenschluager, and Savits in 1889, consisted of a complex of platforms and prosceniums that separated the apron, the middle stage, and a miniature inner stage to facilitate rapid scene changes in Shakespeare's plays (Savits 1890). A direct influence from both of these sources is evident in the production photos of *To Damascus* I and from the interview in *Svenska Dagbladet*, where Strindberg noted that in the production they would 'have only a platform on which the actors appear. Something in the style of Shakespeare's time – all this heavy theatre nonsense which absorbs the stage and makes the play heavy without increasing its value, must be abolished' (Bergman 1967: 16).

Director Emil Grandinson, who had been one of the organisers of the Théâtre de l'Oeuvre's Scandinavian tour in 1894, proved highly receptive to Strindberg's new dramatic style and staging ideas. For *To Damascus* he composed a stage image 'which was divided horizontally to create the impression of two stages, an inner and an outer, joined by three connecting steps' (Marker and Marker 2002: 17). Strindberg found Grandinson's sets beautiful and he was convinced that

> the play could have never been given if we had not gone into simplification. Composed in strict contrapuntal form, [it] ... consists of seventeen tableaux. But allegorizing the pilgrimage the drama marches on until the ninth tableau ... then ... the scenery is reversed to make the drama end on the street corner, where it started. In order to do that quickly, a smaller stage was constructed on stage, contained in an unusually attractive arch painted by Grabow.
>
> (Strindberg 1966a: 292)

Instead of the evocative slide projections originally suggested by Strindberg, a series of realistically painted backcloths by Carl Grabow were used as background for the inner stage. The conventional

Till Damaskus.

Figure 1 Harriet Bosse and August Palme in *To Damascus* I at The Royal
Dramatic Theatre, Stockholm, Sweden, directed by Emil Grandinson
in 1900. Courtesy of the Strindberg Museum, Stockholm, Sweden.

effect of the paintings, however, was offset by Grandinson's staging,
which 'concentrated the whole play on the back stage, raising it,
and in this way giving the impression of distance. The actors
seemed like figures in a relief, which together with half-lighting
gave the impression of unreality' (Bergman 1967: 17). Grandinson
also applied a complex lighting system, presumably inspired by
Lugné-Poë's production of Maeterlinck's *Pelléas and Mélisande* in
Stockholm in 1894, including diminished footlights and concentrated top lighting. Thus, despite some of the failed experiments
carried out by Strindberg and Grandinson, the original production
of *To Damascus* I can be considered avant-garde and epoch making
in the Swedish theatre because of the dream-like effect it achieved

on the whole. In many respects it foreshadowed the German expressionist theatre of the 1910s and 1920s – exemplified by the work of Max Reinhardt – with the successful distortion of reality into shifting nightmarish moods reflecting the main figure's delirious mind.

6 The Intimate Theatre

In 1907 Strindberg embarked on a new theatrical venture that evolved as a practice and aesthetic very different from the naturalistic tendencies of the Scandinavian Experimental Theatre some twenty years earlier. He and the young actor-manager August Falck founded the Intimate Theatre in Stockholm, which opened with the premiere of Strindberg's Chamber Play *The Pelican* on 26 November 1907 and closed in December 1910. The idea was to create an intimate theatre modelled on Max Reinhardt's Kleines Theater and Kammerspiel-Haus, which opened in Berlin in 1902 and 1906 respectively. Reinhardt's programme for the latter, writes Strindberg in his 'Memorandums for the Members of the Intimate Theatre', is indicated by the naming of his project: 'the concept of chamber music transferred into drama' (Strindberg 1966a: 19). According to the original plans, Strindberg and Falck sought to perform modern and classical plays that would fit the intimate atmosphere and the chamber play format: a single 'strong, highly significant motif' (Strindberg 1966a: 19), few characters, and minimal staging requirements. During three years of functioning the Intimate Theatre produced twenty-four Strindberg plays and gave altogether 1,025 performances, some of which comprised of a double bill. The most successful productions were those of *Easter*, with 182 performances, and *Swanwhite* – directed by Strindberg – with 152 performances. Falck's decision to stage Maeterlinck's *The Intruder* in 1910 aroused Strindberg's frustration, which, along with financial difficulties, led to the closing of the theatre (Strindberg 1966a: 12–14).

Figure 2 *The Father* at the Intimate Theatre, Stockholm, directed by August
         Strindberg, 1908. Courtesy of the Strindberg Museum, Stockholm,
         Sweden.

Strindberg and Falck had met in 1906, when the latter produced
Miss Julie for the first time on a public stage in Sweden – eighteen
years after its completion – in the town of Lund, and then
brought the production to Stockholm (see Chapter 11). Falck, who
was a gifted actor-manager and an admirer of Strindberg, had been
the leader of a touring company that included his future wife
Manda Björling, and a group of enthusiastic young actors who
became the founding members of the Intimate Theatre. After a
citywide search for a building, Strindberg and Falck decided to rent
a warehouse at Norra Bantorget, in central Stockholm, which was
at walking distance from Strindberg's residence. The building was
then converted into a small theatre with a stage of six by four metres
and an auditorium seating 161 spectators, painted in light shades of
yellow and green, with deep-green carpeting and brownish-green
seats. The proscenium was flanked by reproductions of Swiss

painter Arnold Böcklin's *The Isle of Life* and *The Isle of Death* respectively. The theatre also consisted of dressing rooms, a ladies' parlour, and a gentlemen's smoking room (Bergman 1967: 25).

The environment and the productions at the Intimate Theatre were geared to realising Strindberg's idea of an art theatre as an alternative to the conventional practice at the Royal Dramatic Theatre and the private commercial houses, where experimentation with new staging methods would serve the high literary quality of the plays. While Falck worked as actor-director and as manager in practical matters, Strindberg assumed the role of adviser and artistic director. Since the company did not include any designers, the two founding partners took care of production design as well. Strindberg's vision for the Intimate Theatre unfolds in the essays collected in the *Open Letters to the Intimate Theatre* (1908), where theoretical and practical considerations are given to all aspects of performance, including acting, gesture, speech, music, scenery, lighting, and costume. Most of all he wanted to make sure that the design and the acting were in complete harmony with both the intimate space and the world of the play. He made a profusion of specific suggestions for scenery and costume solutions for each production and wrote memos to the actors that contained advice on enunciation, movement, tempo, and character analysis.

The bulk of Strindberg's suggestions aimed at achieving atmospheric effects by simple means that would help spectators focus on the central motif of the plays rather than overwhelm them with realistic detail. Watching a rehearsal of *The Pelican*, for instance, he was dissatisfied with Falck's conventionally realistic set and told him that he had envisioned a room with colour and gold in the art nouveau style. Falck listened and, without letting Strindberg know, acquired a set from the workshop of the Opera (Bergman 1967: 27). In *Open Letters* Strindberg describes his surprise at the premiere when he saw exactly what he wished for, 'with furniture in keeping. That was both proper and beautiful, but there was something else in that room, there was atmosphere, a white fragrance of sickroom and nursery' (Strindberg 1966a: 297).

For Strindberg, atmosphere was 'a synonym for poetry', and he also pushed for the elimination of realistic décor because he felt that the Intimate Theatre was 'inadequate for construction on stage' (Strindberg 1966a: 297). After the initial productions, which were still staged in a realistic mode, Strindberg increasingly demanded that they use a stylised *mise en scène*, which would indicate themes and locales emblematically. Since the stage proved too small for magic lantern projections, Strindberg and Falck initiated the so-called drapery stage in several productions, including *Queen Christina* and *Swanwhite*, where the set consisted solely of 'abstract plush draperies' as a standing décor (Strindberg 1966a: 299). Strindberg was equally interested in using simultaneous staging to avoid realism and frequent scene changes. For *To Damascus* I he made sketches where the various locations of the play were suggested on the same set by stylised paintings on the backcloth and on the side wings (Strindberg 1966a: 41). Another important influence for the Intimate Theatre came from *Die Schaubühne der Zukunft* (*The Theatre of the Future* 1905) by Georg Fuchs, playwright, theatre theorist, and the artistic leader of the Munich Art Theatre. In this book Strindberg found effective ways of stylisation, including the idea of the 'relief-stage', which involved actors creating relief-like tableaux on an extremely shallow stage which gave the impression of a dream-like two-dimensional world (Strindberg 1966a: 295–96 and Bergman 1967: 20, 30). But though Falck was sympathetic to Strindberg's ideas, he was a down-to-earth manager whose practical considerations often won out over Strindberg's spirit of experimentation with new styles and technologies. Limited financial resources also contributed to the production style at the Intimate Theatre remaining eclectic, a mixture of innovation and convention.

As for the acting, Strindberg preferred a tight-knit ensemble and felt that the intimacy of the space and the proximity of the performers to the audience required a subdued acting style with subtle gestures and facial expression and well-articulated 'legato' speech. His *Open Letters* and private memos to the actors are rich sources for his views on acting at this time. What is most striking about them is that he discusses acting in musical terms. As the collective name of the Chamber Plays – which he wrote specifically for the

Intimate Theatre – suggests, his ideas on theatre at this time were inspired by Wagner's notion of the total work of art and by Beethoven's sonatas, as much as by Reinhardt's experiments at his Kammerspiele. Strindberg considered speech as the cornerstone of acting and he claimed that 'being the character portrayed intensively is to act well, but not so intensively that he forgets the "punctuation"; then his acting becomes flat as a musical composition without nuances, without piano and forte, without crescendo and diminuendo, accelerando, and ritardando. The actor should know these musical terms and have them constantly in mind, because they say almost everything' (Strindberg 1966a: 132). For Strindberg, the supreme source of the world created on stage is the text of the play. Everything else springs from it and it determines the atmosphere, the scenery, and the 'musical' structure of the performance, i.e. the tone, the mood, the tempo, and the themes. The director functions as an orchestra conductor (Strindberg 1966a: 38) and the actors must focus all their thoughts on their parts and not let themselves be distracted, similarly to musicians who play their instruments and cannot let their thoughts stray from the score without hitting the wrong notes (Strindberg 1966a: 22, 34–36).

The question arises whether Strindberg can be considered a director in a practical sense. When he directed *The Father* in the summer of 1908, he sat quietly in the auditorium during rehearsals and did not instruct actors on the spot. He felt more comfortable giving notes afterwards in writing, yet these notes were extremely observant, specific, practical, and detailed. In the autumn he agreed to direct *Swanwhite*, while Falck was touring in Copenhagen with *Easter*. He started rehearsals with the assistance of the young actor Allrik Kjellgren, planned all the details of scenery, costume, and acting, and again sent a stream of notes to each actor over the rehearsal period.

It is, however, Strindberg's unceasing effort to control and coordinate all aspects of the production for the sake of an artistically unified performance that shows him akin to the theatre artist famously envisioned by Edward Gordon Craig (1872–1966). Strindberg met Craig briefly when the latter visited Stockholm with Isadora Duncan in 1906. Following their meeting, Craig presented

Strindberg with a copy of his portfolio that contained his Shakespeare illustrations and his book *The Art of the Theatre* (Bergman 1967: 18–20). Strindberg also subscribed to Craig's 'attractive periodical' *The Mask* (Strindberg 1966a: 295), in which he found much that responded to his own search for simplified and non-realistic scenery and ways to develop an artistic unity for each production. In *Open Letters* he commented on Craig's 'peculiar ideas', including that he 'wants to have everything presented through the eye, so that the text is to be subordinated. He paints costumes and stylises them, works with lighting effects and even with masks' (Strindberg 1966a: 295). But while Strindberg was taken by many of Craig's ideas, as a playwright he valued most highly the actor's art of the spoken word and rejected Craig's claim of the supremacy of visual composition in the theatre. He envisioned a theatre where the harmony of the performance unfolded from the tones, rhythms, motifs, and movements of the script as if in a polyphonic musical composition.

Both of Strindberg's theatre experiments inspired present-day successors. In Copenhagen director Staffan Waldemar Holm – later Artistic Director of the Royal Dramatic Theatre in Stockholm, 2001–8 – and designer Bente Lykke Møller founded the New Scandinavian Experimental Theatre (Nyt Skandinavisk Forsøgsteater) in 1988, for the centennial of Strindberg and Siri von Essen's original enterprise. Among other experimental productions, they staged there in 1992 a much-acclaimed and highly unconventional *Miss Julie* (see Chapter 11). After the company of the Intimate Theatre disbanded in 1910, its locales were used as trade union offices. Following a long struggle carried on by the Strindberg Society and the Swedish theatre community, Strindberg's theatre was resurrected, refurbished, and reopened to the public on the playwright's birthday, 22 January 2003. The new, modern interior, designed by Sören Brunes, features state-of-the-art lighting equipment, good acoustics, and an intimate auditorium of ninety-three seats surrounding the stage in a semicircle. In the 2007–8 season the Intimate Theatre celebrated its centennial with a production of *The Ghost Sonata* (see Chapter 13). Artistic Director Ture Rangström, grandchild of August Falck's sister Karin Falck and of the actor Allrik Kjellgren from the original company, strives to lead the Intimate Theatre in

'Strindberg's spirit'. For him this highly complex task implies revisiting Strindberg's plays from today's theatrical, cultural, and social perspectives. The Intimate Theatre is also committed to living up to Strindberg's original idea, which at that time remained unrealised, to open the venue for young Swedish dramatists (Rangström 2007: 22–23). And since in those days, says Rangström, the theatre was located in the midst of a working-class district and the Labour Movement's quarters in Stockholm, Strindberg and Falck offered workers discounted tickets. Director Rangström dreams of a time when Strindberg's Intimate Theatre will be a truly free theatre: subsidised, gratis, and open for all (Rangström 2007: 30–31).

PART III

Key plays

Strindberg's contributions as a dramatist are often discussed in the context of two creative phases, separated by his so-called Inferno Crisis (1894–97, see Chapter 1). Martin Lamm's influential work *Strindberg och makterna* (1936) established the Inferno Crisis as a source of the dramatist's aesthetic-religious conversion and a dividing line between the style and outlook of works written before and after *Inferno*. This division stresses the distinct characteristics of each period: the mainly realistic dramaturgy of the early plays exploring contemporary social and psychological issues, and the revolutionary expressionistic techniques of the later plays grappling with metaphysical and existential themes. But to appreciate Strindberg as first and foremost a modern playwright, it is important to recognise some vital continuities in his work. His profound interest in exploring the experience of modernity and presenting his explorations in theatrical form accounts for a lifelong practice of transforming the stage into a laboratory for experimentation. Hence, an all-pervading theatricality throughout Strindberg's work, in the sense that, as we shall see, he distributes his experience to characters in the plays and tests out their conduct in various situations. Strindberg's theatre focuses on individuals whose fates are governed by roles they enact, often unconsciously, as a result of circumstances beyond their control. From the study of dissolving identities and split and vacillating modern souls in the 1880s, he proceeded to exploring the notion of character as a role (Strindberg 1996: 111–16) by the 1890s and created spectacles of metamorphic selves and deceptive masquerades in the 1900s.

7 Naturalism and the modern character

Strindberg's work of the late 1880s and early 1890s signals fundamental societal changes of his time. In the essay 'On Modern Drama and Modern Theatre' (1890), the playwright offers his views on the 'new Naturalistic drama' where 'the action focuses upon life's two poles, life and death, … all those struggles, with their battlefields, cries of pain, the wounded and dead, during which one heard the new view of life as a continuous struggle' (Strindberg 1996: 83–84). This statement sheds light on Strindberg's endeavour in this phase of his career to dramatise the psychological struggles of contemporary characters caught up in a Darwinian battle for the survival of the fittest, with a series of plays including *Comrades* (1886–87), *The Father* (1887), *Miss Julie* (1888), and *Creditors* (1888). He continued to explore naturalistic themes and experiment with new dramaturgical solutions in a series of one-acters including *The Stronger* (1888–89), *Pariah* (1889), *Simoom* (1889), *The First Warning* (1892), *Debit and Credit* (1892), *Facing Death* (1892), *Motherly Love* (1892), *Playing with Fire* (1892), and *The Bond* (1892). Each of these plays deals with what Strindberg believed were the central questions of his time: the apparent shifting of class and gender-roles, sexual and psychological warfare, and the dissolution of traditional notions of identity and family.

While *The Father* dramatises the shock of changing societal and familial hierarchies, *Miss Julie* explores modern 'characterless' souls (Strindberg 1989: 58–59) in a class and sexual context. These plays are not only representative of Strindberg's quest to develop a new and modern mode of drama in the 1880s, but they also established Strindberg's international reputation as both a subversive and a groundbreaking playwright.

The Father (1887)

The Father is the first significant play in the series that demonstrates Strindberg's quest to develop a new dramaturgy for a contemporary subject matter. The play focuses on a shift in the societal power structure represented by the late nineteenth-century bourgeois family. The main conflict is constituted by a clash between the Captain – a scientist and military officer – and his wife, Laura, about the future of their teenage daughter, Bertha, on which subject they have squarely opposing views. The Captain is determined to have Bertha study in the nearby town in order to become a teacher and make an independent living. Conversely, Laura wishes her to stay at home and study painting, for which she is said to have talent. But Bertha, the object of the parents' fight, is consistently silenced; no one is interested in what she thinks, how she feels. She is caught up in her parents' war, identifying with either of them by turn, doomed to internalise their conflict. In 1886 Strindberg had already written a play that he subsequently came to regard a sequel to *The Father*, entitled *Marauder* (1886) – later renamed *Comrades*. Here Bertha is a grown-up woman; an artist married to another artist, with whom she engages in a constant power struggle, not unlike that of her parents in *The Father*.

At the beginning of *The Father* the Captain is fully convinced of his secure position as paterfamilias. He declares that the full authority over the child lies with the father, since women sell their rights in marriage to their husbands, including those over their children. As a scientist, the Captain mocks religion and superstition, and as an atheist, he believes in an afterlife only through one's children. Furthermore, as a military officer, he is used to demonstrating unquestioned authority over others. Yet, as the play progresses, he turns out to possess a highly suggestible mind incapable of adapting to changing circumstances. Laura, on the other hand, is shown as a wilful, demonic woman, plotting to supplant male authority, and she wins the battle because she is the fitter and more adaptable. She instinctively utilises mental suggestion – a form of hypnosis exerted on a waking person – to undo her husband by implanting doubt in his mind about his own fatherhood, and thereby shuttering his self-esteem. When the Captain grows suspicious that Bertha might not be his child, he becomes disturbed and his sense of patriarchal identity gives way. As his fatherhood is brought into question, his faith in an afterlife through children is destroyed and life loses its meaning for him. Once the authority of paternity and the certainty of reason are taken away from him, the Captain's sense of identity dissolves and he goes insane.

The Captain – a pillar of patriarchal society – collapses under the pressure of unpredictable and irrational forces. These are embodied by Laura's use of mental suggestion as a weapon against the rational-minded Captain. The character of Laura embodies the patriarchal fear of the so-called New Woman demanding her share in power. Thus, the meaning of the conflict points beyond the personal and extends into a battle of discourses underlying sexual difference as constructed by the patriarchal order. The foremost scientific and cultural authorities of the time, including Victorian psychiatrists inspired by Darwin, promoted the distribution of power along sexual lines constructing categorical gender roles. These ascribed rational thought, a strong will, and leadership qualities to men and instinctual and irrational behaviour to women (Showalter 1985: 104–7). In *The Father* the 'battle of the brains' (see Chapter 1) becomes a struggle between masculine rationality and feminine irrationality. Such polarising character treatment is a reflection of an all-pervasive, systemic ideology that has helped to sustain patriarchal power relations.

The men in the play are all authority figures; the Captain and the Doctor stand for rational thought, law and order, while the Pastor embodies morality and sanctioned faith. Even the servant, accused of having seduced a maid, is placed in an authority position by his superiors, who automatically brand the pregnant girl as the guilty one. By contrast, the women are all associated with what is regarded whimsical, feminine conduct prompted by irrational beliefs. But gradually a role reversal occurs as the Captain, a man of reason, is driven to madness by 'feminine irrationality', while Laura assumes power position as the head of the family. At the suspenseful conclusion the Captain is tricked by his old nurse into a straitjacket, which visually finalises his regression into a state of complete dependence. His disintegration is the consequence of the loss of the spiritual, moral, and rational foundation – based on the certainty that he is the father of his child – upon which he had built his sense of self. Thus, madness and the irrational in this play signify the loss of 'masculinity', subverting established sexual and cultural hierarchies that had even served as basis for the classical dramatic form. A shift from a traditional to a modern dramatic technique occurs as irrational motivation replaces causation, eliminating the authoritative protagonist of classical drama as the stable and coherent agent of the action.

The play's reception in the Swedish press upon its publication in 1887 is symptomatic of its subversive quality. Critics felt that only a 'sick brain' could have created such an inferior and morally appalling piece. The Captain's doubt about his fatherhood was seen as an affront to all decent housewives and the play was condemned for defiling religion and morality (Strindberg 1984: 282). The piece fared better in the theatre: the world premiere in 1887 at the Casino Theatre in Copenhagen and the Swedish premiere in 1888 at the New Theatre in Stockholm were met with grudging acknowledgements of its powerful effect on the audience (Strindberg 1984: 287–89). And it was *The Father* that established Strindberg's European reputation as an original and provocative modern dramatist through performances in independent theatres, including the Freie Bühne and the Théâtre de L'Oeuvre (see Chapter 4).

When, still in 1887, Strindberg sent a copy of *The Father* to the French writer Émile Zola, the very 'father' of literary and theatrical naturalism, he described the play in an accompanying letter as 'a drama … aiming to show the effect of the inward action at the expense of theatrical tricks' (Strindberg 1992: 243). This focus on the 'inward action' – the psychopathology of the father figure – is what makes the play a truly modern character study. The Captain undergoes an intense emotional turmoil, to the degree of hysteria and finally madness. Laura's instinctive use of mental suggestion that triggers her husband's insanity introduces the irrational and the arbitrary as plot-forwarding impulses and helps to dramatise the modern experience of dissolving identities. That Strindberg realised the novelty of his technique is apparent from his letter to Hans Österling, the publisher who printed *The Father* for the first time in 1887. He characterises the play as 'a modern tragedy … because the battle takes place between souls, a "battle of the brains", rather than with daggers and berry-juice' (Strindberg 1984: 291). With *The Father*, Strindberg took the first step towards drama as a subjective art form.

In favour of this new technique, Strindberg chose to ignore the concrete social milieu, hereditary and environmental factors in motivating the characters' actions. Having read the play in a French translation that Strindberg had sent him, Zola noted a split between the naturalistic claim to an objective and scientific case study and the abstraction of the characters. 'I like it when characters have a complete social identity,' Zola wrote to Strindberg, noting that the Captain 'does not even have a name, and your other characters, who are almost reasonable beings, do not give me the complete sense of life which I demand' (Schumacher 1996: 303).

The abstraction observed by Zola results from the lack of information about any of the characters' past or present circumstances that motivate their actions. The incorporation of unconscious, irrational drives that supplant causal character motivation separates *The Father* from Ibsen's so-called social plays with contemporary subjects – such as *A Doll's House* and *Ghosts* – as well. Ibsen provides ample expository information about the characters' past, where the causes of their present actions are rooted. By contrast, *The Father* and Strindberg's other naturalistic plays jump right into the already heated action. The erratic plot appears to be driven by chance rather than causation. Apart from a general middle-class milieu, we are left in ignorance about the characters' hereditary make-up, their socio-economic environment, and the specific historical moment. Instead, in a masterly vivi-section, Strindberg focuses on the internal processes of a disintegrating mind.

Miss Julie (1888)

In his next play Strindberg was eager to provide a complex background for the main characters and a multiplicity of motives for their actions. In a preface written after the completion of the play he offered a set of interpretive keys aiming to position *Miss Julie* as a model for the modern naturalist playwriting of the future. Here he delineates 'an abundance of circumstances' that bring about Miss Julie's tragic fate, including

> her mother's 'bad' basic instincts; her father's improper bringing up of the girl; her own nature … ; the festive occasion of the Midsummer Night; her father's absence; her period; her preoccupation with animals; the intoxicating effect of the dance; the light summer night; the powerful aphrodisiac influence of the flowers; and finally chance that drives these two people together in a room.
>
> (Strindberg 1998: 58)

In this passage Strindberg is anxious to reassure the reader that he had followed the naturalists' call for characters defined by the triple forces of heredity, environment, and the given moment. Allusions to a rich intellectual foundation – including Darwinist science on biological determinism; the philosophy of Nietzsche and his followers concerning the superiority of an intellectual aristocracy; French psychologists on the complexity and multiplicity of the personality (Törnqvist and Jacobs 1988: 11–19 and Strindberg 1998: xiv–xv) – were meant to ensure the modernity and contemporary relevance of the play. Yet, in *Miss Julie* Strindberg developed a number of techniques of his own which made the play a much more radical departure than *The Father* not only from the naturalists, who demanded case studies of the ordinary and the everyday, but also from classical drama and the mainstream popular theatre of the period. In order to modernise drama in accordance with the demands of contemporary audiences (Strindberg 1998: 56) Strindberg developed an 'experimental formula' which meant 'to make the pain brief [and] let the action spend itself in a single movement' (Strindberg 1992: 291).

Miss Julie is a one-act play consisting of a highly concentrated plot which takes place at the Swedish countryside over the course of Midsummer Eve, when the summer solstice is celebrated throughout Scandinavia. It is set in the kitchen of a Count's manor house, with only three on-stage characters: the Count's daughter Julie, his valet Jean, and his cook and Jean's fiancée, Christine. The Count himself, though he never appears, shapes the plot in several ways. His ubiquitous and fateful presence is made felt through such stage properties as his riding boots and a speaking tube attached to a bell through which he gives orders to the servants from his invisible living quarters located above the kitchen. Jean interacts with these objects as if they stood for the Count himself.

While the Count has left to visit relatives, Julie celebrates Midsummer with the servants and peasants of her father's estate. As Julie and Jean act out their games of mutual attraction–rejection, they are driven into off-stage sexual intercourse by circumstances apparently beyond their control, after which Julie is presented as a 'fallen' woman, both morally and socially, while Jean seems to have gained control over her. He tries to exploit his sexual conquest to rise on the social ladder, suggesting that they flee to Switzerland and open a small hotel. But as the Count returns home and orders his morning coffee through the speaking tube, Jean regresses into servility, while Julie leaves the kitchen with Jean's razor in hand, intent on ending her life.

As with Strindberg's other plays, the subject of *Miss Julie* can be read against the complex background of the dramatist's life. Above all, there is an apparent parallel with the misalliance between Siri von Essen, a noblewoman, and Strindberg, the son of a serving maid – one of his most enduring roles (see Part I). There are several other real-life models for the protagonist. At the time of writing the play Strindberg and his family lodged at the manor house of an eccentric countess in Skovlyst, Denmark, whom he suspected having an illicit affair with her steward – in reality her half-brother. The recent suicide of Swedish novelist Victoria Benedictsson at the Hotel Leopold in Copenhagen – and her previous unsuccessful attempt witnessed by Strindberg – added to the complex of experiences exploited in the play (Törnqvist and Jacobs 1988: 19–26). But the figure of Miss Julie also comprises a self-portrait of the author, who had in *The Maidservant's Son* portrayed Johan, his alter-ego, as a constantly shifting assemblage of influences; a modern, characterless character that he describes in the play's preface (Strindberg 1998: xvii). Thus, again, the autobiographical material helps Strindberg to develop a laboratory experiment where immersion in the lived experience yields findings both in the sphere of dramatic composition and in that of class and sexual politics.

The plot comprises a series of role reversals as the characters struggle for sexual and social dominance over one another in order to achieve a sense of coherence and wholeness within themselves. Both Julie and Jean are split, self-conflicted characters and they lack a coherent identity. Socially, Miss Julie stands above the servant Jean, but, influenced by her plebeian mother, she instinctively strives to 'fall' from her high status and refuses to marry within her social class. By transgressing the socially acceptable codes of conduct – rejecting her aristocratic fiancé and allowing her father's servant to seduce her – Miss Julie revolts against the sexual and social norms of her time. The play thus reveals both gender and class as social constructs enforced by role expectations – not as inborn qualities that mete out one's destiny, as the deterministic philosophy of naturalism would have it. Christine is the only character who feels comfortable in her skin, and as such, she is the least vulnerable. Rather than participating in the action or being affected by it, she is a witness passing moral judgement on what takes place. For some time she is on stage sleeping in a chair, unaware of what is going on around her, providing a naturalistic 'environmental' element for the action.

Julie and Jean tell each other their respective dreams, both of which signal a split self: an unconscious striving towards the repressed other inherent in their psychic constitution. In her dream Julie is sitting on top of a pillar, desperate to get down, but she cannot. She longs to fall but she doesn't have the courage to jump. Yet she feels she cannot have peace until she gets down to the ground, and even further down, below the earth. Jean's dream is about climbing; he wants to reach the top of a giant tree, there to steal the golden eggs from a nest. He knows that if only he could reach the first branch, nothing would stop him from reaching the top.

The dreams have a central dramaturgical function: they both delineate the plot structure, complete with reversal, and foreshadow the ultimate failure of both Julie's and Jean's desire to achieve a unified self. Over the course of the magical Midsummer night, which in Nordic cultures traditionally facilitates playful role reversals, Julie and Jean act out their dreams. But when the consequences of their actions carry over to their realities beyond the beneficial reversibility of holiday games, they realise that they cannot shed their socially sanctioned and internalised roles. What succeeds as play-acting, fails as reality.

The centrality of role play to the plot explains the ups and downs of the characters' interactions and the swift and unexpected emotional changes in both Julie's and Jean's conduct. The second part of the play, for example, starts with a marked change in the manners and appearance of both Julie and Jean as they emerge from Jean's room. Jean immediately begins to play the superior aristocrat, callously ordering about the degraded Julie, who appears filthy, dishevelled, and begging for tenderness. But in a few moments the attitudes and emotional states of both swing to the opposite extreme. Play-acting in *Miss Julie*, then, is a plot-constructing device that not only accommodates the main motifs – split self, sexual and class struggle – but also shapes the dialogue. The characters' internal role conflicts are reflected in their speeches as they keep shifting between their different roles. Julie speaks alternately from the superior position of the estate's mistress and from that of a guilt-ridden, humiliated woman, while Jean treats her with an aristocrat's pride and condescension at one moment, only to kiss her shoe at the next.

Strindberg's preface to the play contextualises the characters' relationships in terms of the struggle for the survival of the fittest. The one more adaptable to shifting circumstances – that is, Jean – will survive. Miss Julie, on the other hand, is presented in the preface from a strongly misogynistic point of view. She is not only a member of a declining social class – that of the aristocracy – but also belongs to a 'degenerate species' of the 'half woman', doomed to extinction. She is a 'type' that offers 'the spectacle of a desperate struggle against nature', and 'a relic of the old warrior nobility that is now giving way to the new aristocracy of nerve and brain'. This new resilient 'species' is represented by Jean (Strindberg 1998: 60–61).

The play itself, however, offers a 'vivisection' (see Chapter 2) of both Julie's and Jean's characters without the ideological trappings of the preface. Like *The Father*, *Miss Julie* focuses on the psychological make-up of the main figures and on the concomitant action. But this approach was at odds with the naturalist demand for an objective plot. Strindberg changed the perspective from which to observe his characters from an external to an internal one. Julie and Jean are driven to one another because of their inner need to resolve their conflicts with themselves and with the world around them. While Jean indeed survives, it is clear that he is just as trapped by internalised social roles as Julie is, and he has no chance of moving up in society. Miss Julie, on the other hand, ultimately regains her dignity as she leaves the kitchen resolutely, with her head raised, while Jean, like Pavlov's dog, keeps cringing in front of the Count's bell and speaking tube.

Strindberg took pride in his dramatisation of the findings of modern psychiatry regarding the multiplicity and complexity of the personality. In his efforts to create modern, internally torn, fragmented characters, he utilised ideas such as mental suggestion, hypnotism, and thought transference, which were vigorously discussed in the psychiatric literature of his day (see Part I). In the concluding sequence of *Miss Julie* he makes use of hypnosis, which many later critics and directors found an outmoded device (see Chapter 11). As they hear the Count return, Julie tries to find courage to kill herself; she begs Jean to order her to do it, as a hypnotist would give an order to a subject. But Jean is already focused on the Count and has fallen out of his superior role. He can only answer to commands, and is unable to utter one. Julie practically hypnotises herself into the deed, telling Jean that she is already 'sleeping', as if in a state of trance. But the significance of this scene lies deeper than just the late nineteenth-century fascination with hypnotism. It is Jean who is hypnotised by the Count's bell and order, and his speech visualises his split self-awareness: 'I can't order you – and now that his Lordship spoke to me ... I can't explain it properly – but – oh, it's this damned lackey sitting on my back' (Strindberg 1998: 109). As Jean is paralysed with fear of the Count, Julie proposes that they switch roles again: Jean must *pretend* to be the Count who gives orders to Jean played by Julie. Thus hypnotism serves to reveal the multiplicity and shifting nature of the characters' utterly fragmented and volatile personalities.

Strindberg defines the play's genre as a naturalistic tragedy (Strindberg 1998: 55). It is a contradictory term, because by making Miss Julie's milieu, upbringing, and hereditary factors responsible for her choices, naturalistic determinism eliminates her liability for bringing about her fate. She is denied even the role of a tragic heroine, which makes her bitterly cry out at the moment of ultimate recognition: 'Who's to blame for all this? My father, my mother, myself? But I have no self of my own. I haven't a thought I didn't get from my father, not an emotion I didn't get from my mother' (Strindberg 1998: 108). If we accept Miss Julie's description of herself, then her destruction cannot be seen as the tragic outcome of her own fateful choices. In classical tragedy the protagonist's downfall is inevitable as a fatal consequence of actions based on free choice, however faulty or short sighted. Instead, both Julie and Jean are victimised by their socially inflicted roles and as a consequence of their missing sense of a coherent self. They are indeed 'characterless' characters, incapable of tragic action that would lend them an identity.

8 Dream-play dramaturgy and modernist allegories

Strindberg's intense revaluation of the artist's relationship to reality during the Inferno Crisis resulted in changed attitudes towards representation. Having returned to Sweden in 1897 after many years abroad, he embarked upon the most productive phase of his career. Several plays of this period dramatise typically modernist modes of experience, including the search for lost identity, the shock of a fragmented, disintegrating self, and the lack of a stable external reality and a rational order of society. From the 1890s Strindberg increasingly rejected the phenomenal world that seemed to offer only deceptive appearances. He found that truth can only be uncovered beneath visible surfaces by way of poetry that taps into deeper layers of the mind. Testifying to Strindberg's continued interest in the psychiatric research of his day, the unconscious in these plays becomes the projecting centre of the drama, the structural organising principle of the experimental works which Strindberg called his dream plays. In the 'Author's Note' to *A Dream Play* (1901) he theorises his new style where he

> attempted to imitate the inconsequent yet apparently logical form of a dream. Everything can happen, everything is possible and probable. Time and place do not exist; on an insignificant basis of reality the imagination spins and weaves new patterns: a blend of memories, experiences, spontaneous ideas, absurdities, and improvisations.
>
> (Strindberg 1998: 176)

It is due to the subjective quality of his later work – where the action, the set, the dialogue, and the characters chart a mental landscape – that Strindberg is credited with creating the modern ego-drama and is hailed as the forerunner of theatrical expressionism. The *To Damascus* trilogy (I, II: 1898, III: 1901) and *A Dream Play* are among the first plays to reject both classical causality and modern realistic devices in favour of a distorted reality presented by means of exaggeration, abstraction, non-linear and ritualised plot, and associatively evolving visual and aural patterns. By these new techniques Strindberg sought to externalise the inner world of the characters and dramatise the workings of the unconscious mind in ways similar to unfolding dream scenarios.

Regardless of Strindberg's avowed allegiance to the naturalists in the 1880s, a number of qualities in the plays of that period already anticipate the later outlook. The torn, vacillating souls in *The Father* and *Miss Julie*, the experimentation with internal conflict, the rapid shifting of extreme emotional states, and the erratic dialogue, though they seem 'natural' and realistic, in fact anticipate the utterly fragmented characters and the abandonment of rational discourse and causal plot in later plays such as the *Damascus* trilogy or *A Dream Play*. The sharp focus on repressed, unconscious psychological drives of mutually interdependent characters in the naturalistic dramas of the 1880s also prefigures the almost stylised power games of the middle-aged couple in *The Dance of Death* (1900) or the concentrated, intimate, and highly subjective form of the later Chamber Plays. But while the pre-Inferno plays are character driven, later works, including the *Damascus* trilogy, *A Dream Play*, and *The Great Highway* (1909), are theme centred and unfold associatively through a succession of verbal, visual, and musical leitmotifs that are varied and repeated throughout the play.

The *To Damascus* trilogy (1898, 1901)

The drama with which Strindberg returned to playwriting following the Inferno Crisis, *To Damascus* I (1898), eventually became the first piece of a trilogy, followed in the same year by part II, and three years later by part III. The title refers to the conversion of St Paul on the road to Damascus (Acts 9:1–31, 22:1–22, 26:9–24). The biblical story recounts how Saul of Tarsus, an avid persecutor of Christians, was blinded by a bright light on his way from Jerusalem to Damascus and heard the voice of Jesus addressing him, whereupon he converted to Christianity and became one of the earliest missionaries, known as Paul the Apostle. By analogy, Strindberg's *Damascus* trilogy follows the spiritual journey of the protagonist, named the Stranger – 'The Unknown One' (Den okände) in literal translation – from an arrogant state of agnosticism, through bouts with an unseen antagonist, 'the Invisible', to the gates of a cloister in the high mountains where he is about to enter.

Because of its autobiographical aspect the trilogy has often been read and performed as a work about Strindberg's religious conversion or, in a somewhat broader sense, as a dramatisation of the experiences described in the novel *Inferno*, including the playwright's second marriage, with Frida Uhl, and his spiritual, occult, and psychotic experiences during the crisis years (Strindberg 1979: 7–9, Ollén 1972: 59–61, Strindberg 1971b: 14–15). Yet, to appreciate the work as a bold and pioneering exploration of the modern subjectivity, there is no need to rely on the biography. With a typically Strindbergian gesture, the playwright in these new plays exploits his own life to work out new techniques that help externalise internal action. The Stranger – unknown even to himself – is shown undertaking an internal journey, engaged in fabricating an identity from the fragments of his former self and memories, and with the help of narratives, archetypes, and his imagination. While the three parts of *To Damascus* can be understood and performed either individually or in sequence as a whole, part I is the dramatically most fully developed and most effective play of the three and therefore it is most often staged alone.

The treatment of the action, setting, dialogue, and characters in *To Damascus* I departs from the naturalistic dramaturgy of the previous period. The scenes combine both realistic and abstract details, but there are some vaguely odd or blatantly symbolic elements even in the seemingly most natural milieus, creating a dreamlike atmosphere. Hallucinatory and dream effects evoke a sense of 'half-reality' (Strindberg 1992: 624), unprecedented in the earlier drama, which makes the Stranger constantly question the soundness of his senses. The people he encounters seem unreal to him and sometimes he needs to touch them in order to believe that they exist. They emerge out of nowhere and they all have some mysterious connection with the Stranger. The Lady, who eventually elopes with him, seems to be materialising from his thoughts; he encounters a Beggar who wears a scar on his forehead at the same spot as the Stranger; he meets a madman named Caesar, the very nickname the Stranger bore in his youth; and when he ends up in an asylum, he is confronted with a company of ghostlike figures resembling people who played a role in his earlier life. In contrast with the naturalistic plays, these characters lack both individuality and proper names; they seem to embody aspects of the Stranger's subjectivity – his unconscious fears, desires, memories, and guilt feelings – rather than living a life of their own. They are pieces in a jigsaw puzzle with which the Stranger attempts to assemble his identity, which, as his name suggests, is unknown to him. Thus, while structurally *To Damascus* I resembles a medieval passion play, it unfolds following an abstract, repetitious pattern representing recurrent themes, like musical leitmotifs, in the Stranger's unconscious.

Contrary to the objective sets of naturalism and realism, even the scenery becomes a continuation of character, reflecting the protagonist's states of mind. It was Swedenborg's theory of correspondences – insisting that the spiritual spheres are reflected in the natural world (Sprinchorn 1982: 106–7) – that helped Strindberg externalise internal processes on stage. The Stranger is pursued by visions and hallucinations, including haunting images of his enemies, of hell and purgatory, or the menacing tune of a funeral march. He perceives his fears, guilt, and redemption laid out in the landscapes he passes, or materialise in the Lady's crocheting, in the wallpaper in a hotel room, or in an infernal black smithy, all of which possess a physical stage reality. It is, then, with Swedenborg's guidance that Strindberg developed a technique to show the characters, time, place, and dialogue as simultaneously real and symbolic, objective and subjective. The stage effects are conceived in such a way that the audience experiences the same uncertainties as the Stranger; the same sense of vacillation between what is real and what is unreal. Yet, there is always a seemingly realistic starting point from which the spectator is drawn into subjective space. In part I, for example, we meet the Stranger at the street corner in a small town where we see a tavern on one side and a church on the other, and this is the place we return to at the conclusion, when he is discovered sitting on the same street-bench as in the beginning, writing with his cane in the dust of the street. Thus, while the set that frames the action seems to be a 'real' location, by the end we are left uncertain whether the Stranger has moved through all the stations of his journey or whether we have been made to contemplate the evolving internal landscapes of his mind – the mind of the artist who constructs reality by means of poetry. In a letter to Swedish author Gustaf af Geijerstam, Strindberg himself describes the structural principles of his new play:

> The art lies in the composition which symbolizes 'The Repetition' that Kierkegaard[1] speaks of: the action unrolls forwards to the asylum; there it kicks against the pricks and rebounds back through the pilgrimage, the relearning, ... until it begins again at the same point as the action stops, and where it began. You may not have noticed how the settings unroll backwards from the Asylum, which is the spine of a book that shuts upon itself and encloses the action. Or like a snake that bites its own tail.
> (Strindberg 1992: 624)

Early on, the Stranger confides to the Lady that he is a poet, and indeed, he acts like the author of a play within the play, which he invents step by step. He declares that he not only plays with death, but 'I play with life – I was a writer, you know ... and there are moments when I doubt life has more reality than my poems' (Strindberg 1979: 22). Having no sense of the real and of a coherent identity, the Stranger creates reality by inventing the play of his life, striving to retrieve a self by acting out roles in it. To begin with, he promptly involves the Lady in his life. He decides to call her Eve and goes on to determine her age and flesh out her personality.

He talks to her as a director who explains the role to an actor. She is not an independent human being for the Stranger, but a carrier of roles she is supposed to play in his story.

To Damascus exploits mythic structures that chart the workings of the unconscious. The Stranger dramatises himself by identifying with various mythical characters. Christ's passion and Saul's transformation into St Paul are his two major narratives to enact. He assumes these identities as he passes what are visually and verbally referred to as Stations of the Cross. When he then traces his steps backwards, in a reverse order, his course indicates a process of conversion. Thus, both of these archetypal stories are integrated in the composition, but their treatment is distinctly modern. By having the protagonist re-enact them, Strindberg succeeds in externalising intra-psychic conflicts and turning them into a ritual performance.

In search of formal devices that could communicate the modern experience, Strindberg found models in the medieval theatre. The so-called morality and passion plays were allegorical representations – communicating abstract ideas through story and character – of the Christian doctrine in accessible and entertaining forms. But while Strindberg borrowed the journey structure from such models, in his world the universal and eternal spiritual laws are no longer available to govern the lives of individuals. Rather, as his characters move through physical space, they actually tread the paths of inner mental landscapes or lose their way in the depths of their own psyche. With the *Damascus* trilogy Strindberg developed a new genre, the modern passion play or 'station drama' (Szondi 1987: 26), which was to become a model for the German Expressionist playwrights of the 1910s and 1920s, including Georg Kaiser, Ernst Toller, and Walter Hasenclever, and for Eugene O'Neill's early expressionistic plays, such as *The Emperor Jones* (1920) and *The Hairy Ape* (1921).

Since the world premiere of the first part in 1900 (see Chapter 5) even this work has had a remarkable stage history. In 1937 acclaimed Swedish director Olof Molander staged part I at the Royal Dramatic Theatre in Stockholm, focusing on 'the autobiographical and the religious motif', with both the Stranger (Lars Hanson) and the Madman Caesar wearing a Strindberg mask (Bark 1981: 135). The church entrance as a constant element in the

Figure 3 Berit Kornhill and Dana Marouf in *Strindberg on the Track – To Damascus* I, Gnistor (Sparks) Theatre Group, performed in a Stockholm subway car, 1997. Photo by Ove Westerberg, courtesy of Dana Marouf.

scenery alluded to the religious framework, while the staging shifted back and forth between realistic and dream-like sequences (Bark 1981: 137). In conjunction with his 1974 production of the first two parts Ingmar Bergman claimed that in '*To Damascus* we wander in an immense soul-landscape – Strindberg's' (Bark 1981: 167). But rather than making up actor Jan-Olof Strandberg to resemble Strindberg, Bergman sought to capture moments of transition from reality to dream and to create dream-like transformation scenes with the help of a revolving stage (Bark 1981: 168–71). In 1997 Kurdish director and actor Dana Marouf, residing in Sweden, and Swedish actress Berit Kornhill introduced a novel approach with their production of part I at the Strindberg Festival in Stockholm. *Strindberg on the Track – To Damascus* I was performed in one of the cars of a working underground line in Stockholm by a cast of six members of the international theatre group Sparks. When the company could not find a locale for the performance, the Stockholm Public Transportation Bureau stepped in as a sponsor. The hour-and-a-half-long performance unfolded twice a day before forty-one spectators during the course of a round trip between the Royal Gardens in the inner city and Akalla station in the suburbs. The sign indicating the train's direction read 'To Damascus'. The company devised a frame story in which an immigrant (Marouf) and a Swedish woman (Kornhill) meet on the underground, and connect through Strindberg. The actual Damascus story was enacted as a play-within-the-play where the actors shifted roles, Kornhill playing the Stranger – a foreigner – and Marouf the Lady.[2] Strindberg's piece thus assumed topical significance as an auto-biographical piece for the performers and as an exploration of questions of identity, immigration, encounters with 'the Other' (the Unknown One) in contemporary society, and on the healing power of the theatre.

The Dance of Death I and II (1900)

At first sight the world of *The Dance of Death* seems similar to *The Father* in both form and subject: it presents the marriage woes of a middle-aged couple, in which their daughter plays a central role, set in a contemporary middle-class milieu. But upon a closer look differences from the naturalist style become clear. *The Dance of Death* I, which was originally conceived as a single play, is another post-Inferno work that utilises medieval imagery while using specific details of the author's life-experience as a springboard to dramatise existential situations. In addition to the spiritual bouts of his Inferno Crisis (1894–97), which were still haunting the playwright's mental universe when he wrote *The Dance of Death*, the recent deaths of close friends and acquaintances affected him deeply. In his notes while composing the play Strindberg recorded his interest in the process of dying and the struggle with death. Another related theme was introduced with the figure of the vampire, which Strindberg thought of as a metaphor not for the dead that haunt the living, but rather for a dying person who clings to life by interfering with others' destinies, taking control of others' lives, and living vicariously through them (Brandell 1983–89, vol. 4: 120–21).

The play's title already points beyond realism and evokes an archetypal image. It refers to the medieval trope of the *danse macabre* associated with allegorical representations, in which a personified Death leads people, joining hands in a solemn dance, to the grave. Whether in the form of church murals, sermons, or theatrical presentations, the motif of the dance of death stressed the equality of all before death, regardless of rank, age, or gender. The setting of part I also brings to mind the allegorical framework of medieval morality plays. In *The Castle of Perseverance* (c1450), for instance, Mankind's castle is situated in the centre of a circle surrounded by water, and the action represents Mankind's progress from birth through death to the Last Judgement. Similarly, Strindberg's play takes place in a circular fortress tower on an island surrounded by the sea. The island is nicknamed Little Hell, and the fortress used to be a prison. The action describes a circular pattern as it concludes by returning to the starting point: the couple sitting alone in their drawing-room. Thus the action, the dialogue, and the set are constructed so that they can be read in several different ways: both realistically and allegorically. It is nonetheless a modernist allegory, presenting the characters' existential predicament rather than a religious doctrine dramatised by the medieval theatre.

The battling spouses, the former actress Alice and the artillery captain Edgar, were inspired by multiple real-life models, including Strindberg's sister Anna and her husband Hugo von Philp, with whom the dramatist, like cousin Kurt in the play, regularly spent time upon returning from abroad (Brandell 1983–89, vol. 4: 115–21, Strindberg 1998: xxi). Yet the realistic perspective is undercut by the dialogue, already with the first exchange:

CAPTAIN: Won't you play something for me?
ALICE:　... What shall I play?
CAPTAIN: What *you* like.
ALICE: You don't like my repertoire.
CAPTAIN: Nor you mine.

(Strindberg 1998: 113)

This overture introduces the leitmotif of playing, which is then varied throughout the play. The dialogue of part I is constructed of sequences in which the characters are playing games, acting out roles, or talking about playing. They play cards, Alice plays the piano, and Edgar dances – all in order to fill time and forget the monotony of their isolated death-in-life. When they run out of ideas for what to play, they lament the boredom and repetitiveness of their interactions and their lives. They are reinvigorated only when Alice's cousin Kurt, arriving to take a position as quarantine officer on the island, turns up in their fortress. Their domestic squabbles turn into a stage play where Kurt is forced into the role of spectator and unwilling participant. Edgar also has a predilection for rewriting the past, dramatising his own and others' lives. Deliberately ignoring the facts, for example, he constantly admonishes Kurt for abandoning his children. Thus fictionalising reality, he creates roles to play while he steals into others' lives to escape the emptiness of his own. When Kurt tells Edgar, 'I've noticed how you invented a life for yourself and those around you,' he replies: 'There comes a moment when the ability to invent, as you call it, ends. And then reality is revealed in all its nakedness! – It's terrifying!' (Strindberg 1998: 167).

The traditionally causal plot yields to a series of verbal duels where much of the dialogue consists of recurring clichés or key lines of the characters' roles within their role. Language has no information value, nor does it reveal the ideas or emotions of the speaker. On the contrary, Edgar and Alice use speech to conceal their feelings and falsify information. Alice even gets into the habit of 'translating' Edgar's speeches, guessing the hidden intent behind what is being said, not unlike an actor would analyse a character's lines in a play. Strindberg's claustrophobic universe and metatheatrical treatment of character, plot, and dialogue came to deeply inspire twentieth-century European and American theatre, anticipating such developments as existentialist drama and the Theatre of the Absurd. To mention just a few specific examples, the impact of *The Dance of Death* I can be traced to Sartre's presentation of the proverbial 'hell is other people' in *No Exit* (1941); to the non sequitur language and ritualised plots of Beckett's early plays *Waiting for*

Godot (1952) and *Endgame* (1957); to *Play Strindberg* (1969), Dür-
renmatt's comedy of a bourgeois marriage tragedy set in a stylised
boxing ring; or to the marital hell of Edward Albee's *Who's Afraid
of Virginia Woolf?* (1961–62; see Robinson 1998: 92–111).

In their isolation, Alice and Edgar are set apart from the flow of
time and from any reality outside the microcosm of their relationship.
At the conclusion of part I they find themselves back in the same
position as in the opening scene, preparing to celebrate their silver
wedding. The circular plot structure suggests the course of their life,
dragging on in perpetual cycles as they are caught up in the clichés
and repetitions of existence as living dead, without any possibility
for growth or change. But because of Edgar's forgiving, reconcilia-
tory gesture at the conclusion, part I has been read as another religious 'conversion' play, where, following his bouts with death, the
protagonist arrives at a point of reversal, entering a phase of
atonement. According to this reading, a profound spiritual change
takes place in Edgar's character in a mute scene during which he
divests himself of possessions that had bound him to a material
existence. This scene dramatises what the Swedish mystic
Swedenborg describes as a process of purgation or 'vestation'
(Sprinchorn 1982: 112–13). Yet, the character's overt theatricality
and the closing of the plot upon itself, as if the couple were doomed
to run the cycles of their marital hell forever, do not suggest religious transcendence.

The Dance of Death II, the sequel that Strindberg wrote to satisfy
the request of his German translator for a brighter outlook
(Strindberg 1998: xxiii), develops one of the secondary themes of
part I. Part II was originally titled 'The Vampire' (Strindberg 1988a:
247), in reference to Captain Edgar's nature, which already in part I
is described by Alice as 'seizing hold of other peoples' destinies,
sucking excitement out of other people's lives, ordering and arran-
ging for others, because his own life is quite devoid of interest'
(Strindberg 1988a: 152). In part II, then, this vampire nature comes
to full bloom as the circle of people to exploit is extended. Here
there is no trace of Edgar's religious conversion; on the contrary, he
returns as a menacing force, striving to control and ultimately
destroy others, most notably Kurt. Strindberg's 'vampire' is a

metaphor of the self as a hollow shell that keeps on living by appropriating others' selves. The Captain's actions do not convey any sense of atonement or preparation for death; instead, he thrives on what he extorts from Kurt. His death is brought about by a *deus ex machina*: his daughter Judith's unexpected revolt against her father's scheme to marry her off to the old Colonel. As opposed to Bertha in *The Father*, Judith refuses to be silenced or sacrificed in her parents' battle. She changes the script and writes her own destiny, which is also her father's doom.

The reception of *The Dance of Death* cycle shows a pattern similar to many of Strindberg's most innovative plays. It was condemned by Swedish critics upon its publication in 1901 as a work 'more hideous … and annoying' than anything Strindberg had ever written (Ollén 1961: 335). The world premiere of both parts took place in 1905 at the Residenztheater in Cologne, Germany, directed by Fritz Kremien, with Elimar Striebeck and Helene Reichers in the lead roles. It was a highly successful production that subsequently toured in forty German cities over the winter season of 1905–6. The Swedish premiere at the Intimate Theatre in 1909 turned into one of the company's great triumphs, with eighty-five performances (after twenty-two performances of part I, both parts were given together) and tours in the provinces. One of the most famous productions of both parts was directed by Max Reinhardt in 1912 at the Deutsches Theater in Berlin, with Gertrud Eysoldt and Paul Wegener, while at the Swedish tour at the Royal Dramatic Theatre in 1915 Rosa Berten played Alice. In both Sweden and Germany, Wegener was long remembered for his riveting performance as Captain Edgar. In Reinhardt's directorial interpretation no religious conversion occurred in part I. The performance began and concluded in the same set, as Edgar and Alice were seated far apart from each other, with their backs to the audience, glaring out into nothingness (Ollén 1961: 335–38 and Strindberg 1966a: 12–13).

A Dream Play (1901)

While *To Damascus* I, as Strindberg's first 'dream play', is a groundbreaking work, *A Dream Play* is an exquisite stage poem that transcends the experimental phase. It presents the story of the daughter of the Indic god Indra who, driven by her desire to learn about the human condition, incarnates as the earthly woman Agnes. Here, on 'the densest and heaviest / Of all the spheres that wander in space' (Strindberg 1998: 178), she observes and experiences the contradictions of earthly existence, including those of joy and pain, spirit and matter, love and hate, cruelty and compassion: the irreconcilable tension between opposites that seems to perpetuate human suffering. Her guides and partners on the journey include the Officer, the Lawyer, and the Poet; nameless but distinct characters, or rather types, that can also be seen as three different sides of the same person – the naive and credulous, the bitter and resigned, and the rebellious and always striving aspects of the mind. The naturalist notion of the 'characterless characters' (see Chapter 7) is taken here to an extreme, and as Strindberg explains in his Author's Note to the play, the characters 'split, double, multiply, evaporate, condense, disperse, and converge' as they would do in dreams (Strindberg 1998: 176).

Indra's Daughter/Agnes is herself the most metamorphic figure, in whom autobiographical elements mingle with multiple mythological and fairy-tale allusions. Character complexity here does not involve a realistic representation of the kind of psychologically rounded personalities developed, for example, by Ibsen in his so-called social plays such as *Ghosts* (1881), but rather, an assemblage of fragments of personal and cultural memories and narratives that are patched together in such figures as the protagonist of *A Dream Play*. Strindberg wrote the part for his young wife, actress Harriet Bosse, in whose features he admired a sort of 'oriental' beauty, which might have provided the initial impulse to make the Daughter an Indic goddess. In their life together Strindberg cast his wife in the role of his saviour, who would reconcile him 'with the world through woman' (Strindberg 1998: xxv). In September 1901 he wrote to Harriet, who had left him while pregnant: 'I am writing "The Growing Castle" [an early title for *A Dream Play*], grand, beautiful, like a dream. ... It is of course about you – Agnes – who will free the Prisoner from the castle' (Strindberg 1992: 685). The letter illustrates how, from 'an insignificant basis of reality'

(Strindberg 1998: 176), Strindberg made a leap of the imagination and placed the Daughter in a composite cultural-mythological context. Her first mission on earth is to free the Officer imprisoned in the Growing Castle, which establishes her both as a spiritual saviour and as a social rebel who attempts to open forbidden doors. Over the course of her earthly journey Indra's Daughter is called Agnes. To add another layer of signification, Agnes means 'lamb', which is a clear reference to Christ, the sacrificial 'lamb of god' (*Agnus Dei*). Besides all these different personae encoded in her figure, the Daughter also plays various earthly roles as she is drawn into the action and, marrying the Lawyer, becomes a wife and a mother; roles that she eventually comes to reject.

While in her various roles the Daughter is made to figuratively multiply, she also transforms herself into others and, surrendering herself in a gesture of compassion, becomes their surrogate. In the cathedral scene, for example, she begins to play the organ. But instead of organ tones, lamenting human voices are heard. She serves as a musical instrument, letting the voices of suffering people resound through her. In the scene toward the end of the play at Fingal's Cave, which is said to represent the ear of Indra, she recites the Poet's supplication to the gods directly from his mind. Such actions dramatise her recurring line, 'Human beings are to be pitied' (Strindberg 1998: 187), which carries the central theme of the play. The verbal phrase is elaborated with the help of associatively and rhythmically evolving situations, which repeat and modify the theme. In a note to Victor Castegren, director of the world premiere of the play in 1907, Strindberg explained his 'dream play' technique in musical terms:

> As far as the loose, disconnected form of the play is concerned, that, too, is only apparent. For on closer examination, the composition emerges as quite coherent – a symphony, polyphonic, now and then in the manner of a fugue with a constantly recurring main theme, which is repeated and varied by the thirty odd parts in every key. … The vocal parts are strictly arranged, and in the sacrificial scene of the finale, everything that happened passes in review, with the themes repeated once

again, just as a [person's] life with all its incidents, is said to do at the moment of death.

(Strindberg 1998: 300)

The speeches of the constantly metamorphosing characters are thus traversed by shifting points of view, which contributes to what Strindberg calls the 'polyphonic' musical structure of the work as a whole. Just as important is the flexible treatment of theatrical space. *A Dream Play* is an episodic piece with frequent scene changes, suggested by simple, non-realistic means, such as changes in lighting or drawing aside a screen to reveal a hidden tableau. The stage directions request the use of free-standing set pieces in varying functions, for example, a tree turning into a coat rack or a door into a cabinet. It was important for Strindberg to create dream-like transformations on the open stage and indicate transitions between the scenes without heavy theatre machinery, in order to maintain the fluidity of the performance and not to 'materialise' the dream too much (see Chapter 12). Such metamorphic treatment of stage space emulates the instantaneous and seemingly illogical changes of milieus in dreams. As the Daughter enters the miraculous Growing Castle she finds herself inside the Officer's parental home. From this point she keeps moving inside this flexible, kaleidoscopic space where the subsequent locations – the opera, the Lawyer's office, the cathedral, Fingal's Cave, Foul Port, and Fair Haven – unfold as if each time another curtain, covering hidden recesses of the mind, was drawn aside. By the conclusion of her journey she finds herself at the same spot from where she started: in front of the Growing Castle. In the final move she re-enters the burning castle, only to cast off her earthly frame and ascend to the heavens, which in a dream context could suggest awakening. Such a reading corresponds with the Daughter's explanation of the 'riddle of the universe' that 'the world, life, and [people] are … only phantoms, an illusion, a dream image' (Strindberg 1998: 243). In such de-materialised space, locations, people, and fragments of conversations emerge and re-emerge seemingly randomly; characters grow old, only to be rejuvenated again, and the linden tree loses its leaves and regains them in a few seconds, defying the notion of linear time. Each scene is composed as a miniature play-within-the-play, with Agnes looking on as a spectator and, drawn into the situation, often becoming an actor in it, which enhances the overall dream effect.

In devising the dream-like universe of *A Dream Play* Strindberg drew on a blend of sources, including readings on Hinduism and Buddhism and Western interpretations of Indian metaphysics (Carlson 1996: 297–99). Early in the nineteenth century Schopenhauer had seen the world as a mere representation, entirely conditioned by the subject; in his main work, *The World as Will and Representation* (1818–19), he borrowed the Indic concept of Maya, the veil of deception, to express the illusory quality of perceived reality. Other sources of inspiration, as Strindberg noted in his letter to director Castegren, included such works of the classical theatre as the great philosophical allegory of Calderon's play, *Life is a Dream* (1635), and Shakespeare's *The Tempest* (c. 1610–11), where Prospero remarks, 'We are such stuff as dreams are made on' (Strindberg 1998: 299). *A Dream Play* is thus criss-crossed by multiple mythical, philosophical, psychological, and literary narratives, creating a pastiche of allusions that produces a polyphonic text, even if one is not familiar with the underlying sources. The modernity of *A Dream Play* lies not in the originality of its themes and motifs but in the innovative ways of their combination that allowed the playwright to dramatise the experience of an incomprehensible world of contradictions, where human beings may no longer rely on a higher order or divine providence.

But this poetic probing into the human condition and metaphysical suffering is interlaced with an exploration of social injustice. Almost every scene is wrought with pain inflicted by inequities and oppression. The Officer's home echoes Strindberg's childhood memories described in *The Maidservant's Son* with his dying mother and unjust punishments; serving maids, including the pasting Christine and the abused wife Lina, haunt the stage; the pain of the ostracised Ugly Edith and the life of the Billposter spent in vain hope, are memorialised in poignant scenes; the political squabbles of the academic faculty and 'the right-thinking people' who stone designated scapegoats are venomously satirised; and the Lawyer who defends the needy is shown as an outcast. The central metaphor of the play, that beauty – that of the flowers surrounding the Growing Castle – is rooted in and nurtured by dirt, is echoed by the social theme, for instance in the scene with the coal-heavers at the Mediterranean. This sequence casts light on the ultimate contradiction that while society rests on the coal-heavers' sweat, and would collapse without their work, they are still detested and denied even the right to drown themselves in the ocean, because the beach is owned by the idle upper classes. Interestingly, Strindberg felt it important to insert this scene following the completion of the rest of the manuscript in November 1901. The addition may have been inspired by the increasing political unrest in Stockholm, which culminated in workers' rioting and general strike in April and May 1902 (Strindberg 1988b: 146).

The themes of sexual inequity and gender roles in patriarchal society are addressed as well. Like Miss Julie, Agnes rebels against her role as a woman relegated to the domestic sphere. She transgresses taboos by forcing open doors forbidden for women: the door to exit the family home and the door to the riddle of the universe. By leaving home and family to see after the problems of humanity, she enters the public realm traditionally reserved for men. Her attempts to liberate humanity, however, are rejected and denounced by the powers that be, including the political and cultural establishment. Depending on the perspective from which one views her figure, her fate can be seen in several different ways. If her death signifies the elimination of flesh and the awakening of the spirit, as traditional interpretations would have it, she is then sublimated and reintegrated in the mythicised structure of the patriarchal order. If she is seen as a female Christ figure, sacrificed vicariously for the sins of humanity, she assumes the conventional role of self-sacrificing woman. For Strindberg, partially at least, she represented Harriet Bosse, leading the unconventional life of an artist, who even rivals with the Poet. As such, one can see her as a woman victimised and punished for her daring to transgress social norms. Her ritual death catapults her from the earth as the etherealised 'other'. From her perspective, *A Dream Play* is Agnes's dream of freedom that ends with her awakening to a bleak reality.

Upon its publication in 1902 *A Dream Play* prompted mixed reactions. Some reviewers were fascinated by its poetic intensity and by the fluidity of ingenious dream scenes, while others felt that this was Strindberg's 'most violent, most illogical, most faulty piece, but also his most enthralling and above all psychologically most interesting' one (Strindberg 1988b: 151). Another critic dismissed it as an entirely formless work which must have been written without any plan or conception, and warned readers that 'the dreamlike presentation can make many naïve souls believe that there is a deeper meaning in the empty play of images' (Strindberg 1988b: 151–52). Meanwhile Strindberg sought to get producers interested, but without success. In 1903 he tried to convince Hjalmar Selander, director of Folkets Hus (The People's House) theatre, that the play could be done using only twelve backdrop screens for sciopticon projections and a few partitions which, when drawn aside, could indicate scene changes without lowering the curtain. Regardless, Selander found it safer to stage Strindberg's older fairy-tale play *Lucky Per's Journey* (1881–82). In 1906 Strindberg added a Prologue: a dialogue in the ether between the Daughter and her invisible divine father, Indra. In anticipation of a production he felt that this frame story would help the audience to better understand the dramatic situation. But he had to wait until 1907 for the premiere (see Chapter 12) of his 'most beloved drama, the child of [his] greatest pain' (Strindberg 1988b: 152).

Notes

1 Søren Kierkegaard (1813–55), Danish philosopher. On his significance for the later work of Strindberg see Sprinchorn 1982: 80–81, 106–8.
2 Interview with director and actor Dana Marouf, Stockholm, Sweden, 11 July 2007.

9 The last sonatas

> It's probable that I am now entering upon something new. I long
> for the light, have always done so, yet, have never found it. ... My
> whole life seems to me as if it had been staged for me, so that
> I might both suffer and portray it.
>
> (Strindberg 1992: 737)

In this letter to his German translator, Emil Schering, Strindberg
alludes to the new plays he was in the process of composing for the
Intimate Theatre (see Chapter 6). Four of the five pieces that he would
call his Chamber Plays (Strindberg 1992: 735–39) – *Thunder in the
Air*, *The Burned House*, *The Ghost Sonata*, and *The Pelican* – were
completed during the spring of 1907. To these works, which he
referred to in a letter as his 'Last Sonatas' (Strindberg 1992: 735) and
provided with opus numbers, he added *The Black Glove* in 1909 as
Opus 5. In his 'Memorandums to the members of the Intimate
Theatre from the Director' (1908) Strindberg expands on the distinct
characteristics of this group of plays. He mentions Max Reinhardt,
who a year before opened 'the Kammerspiel-Haus, which by its very
name indicates its real program: the concept of chamber music
transferred to drama'. He further explains 'what is meant by chamber
plays'. One must 'seek the strong, highly significant motif' and

> try to avoid in the treatment all frivolity, all calculated effects,
> places for applause, star roles, solo numbers. No predetermined
> form is to limit the author, because the motif determines the

form. Consequently: freedom in treatment, which is limited only by the unity of the concept and the feeling for style.

(Strindberg 1966a: 19)

An analogy with music in each play is provided by a few over-arching themes, which, like musical leitmotifs in a Beethoven sonata, are repeated and varied in different contexts throughout the consecutive 'movements' (equivalent to acts) of the piece. But the 'chamber' in the Chamber Plays also connotes Strindberg's novel treatment of space. Each piece takes place in a modern city dwelling; a middle-class apartment house with 'chambers' piled up in an apparently random fashion, yet filled with lives utterly entwined. These chambers are sometimes invaded by outsiders, who eventually turn out to be related to those already in the house (*Thunder in the Air*, *The Burned House*, *The Ghost Sonata*); they are laid out vertically, suggesting a pile of entangled destinies (*Thunder in the Air*, *The Black Glove*); stretched out horizontally as a labyrinthine network of interconnected recesses (*The Ghost Sonata*); or their entrails are exposed, gutted by fire (*The Burned House*). They are invariably constructed with a view of death.

The themes explored in each Chamber Play are revealed gradually through evocative patterns of visual and aural metaphors that replace causal plot and realistically motivated character development. The first movement presents a realistic tableau; either an urban street scene (*Thunder in the Air*, *The Burned House*, *The Ghost Sonata*) or an interior (*The Pelican* and *The Black Glove*); both of which were recognisable for contemporary Stockholm audiences. Each initial image contains an element that turns into the central metaphor of the play, its significance elaborated throughout the action. *Thunder in the Air* opens with the image of a modern house façade with open windows, through one of which an elderly gentleman can be seen sitting at his dining table. We soon find out that he has withdrawn from the outside world to spend the rest of his days in quiet introspection, preparing for death. The initial stage image thus captures a moment of transition between outside and inside, life and death, presenting the leitmotif to be elaborated by the ensuing action.

The opening image of *The Burned House* shows the ruins of an apartment building ravaged by fire, seen from the street but exposing what remained of the interior. The dialogue then makes clear that the suburb where the action takes place is called the Swamp and lies halfway between the city and the cemetery. A restaurant, called The Last Nail, is also part of the set. The main character is the Stranger who returns home from America only to find his childhood home in ashes. But behind the ruins of the house he beholds an orchard that has burst into bloom as a result of the heat from the fire. The opening tableau visualises the stations of life's journey from the Paradise of childhood, through the fires of Inferno – which Strindberg now identified with earthly life – to the final resting station.

The Ghost Sonata again presents an image of a house façade seen from the street, but with interior scenes visible through the open windows. Simultaneously, we hear church bells ringing and the siren of a steamboat announcing a journey. And indeed, the trajectory of the plot describes a journey from the exterior view, through interior spaces of the house, to the concluding image of the 'Island of the Dead', represented by Arnold Böcklin's painting, which engulfs the room where a young lady has just died.

The Pelican's set reveals a family living-room with the dead father's rocking chair, which later rocks by itself, awakening the Mother's guilty conscience. At the conclusion of the play, as the house is engulfed in flames, the Mother plunges to her death from a window while her emotionally and physically starved Daughter and Son embrace, awaiting 'summer vacation': their awakening from the horrible dream of life to a better world hereafter.

The Black Glove (1909) is a Christmas story in verse and five acts. It begins in the vestibule of again another modern apartment house, where the elderly taxidermist finds the lost glove of a young woman living in the same building. By the conclusion both of them have undergone a series of trials and tribulations, and he dies in his attic room while she, having learned humility, finds her lost infant again in the nursery. The action revolves around the glove, visualising the entanglement of the fates of everyone living in the house (the old man turns out to be the young woman's long-lost father, for example).

In each Chamber Play what initially seems a realistic situation turns into a symbolic rite of passage throughout a series of inter-linked liminal spaces. The images do not simply provide visual backgrounds to the plot, but rather, they create the plot, signalling stations over the course of journeys of transition from outside to inside, from dreaming to awakening, from conscious to uncon-scious, from illusion to reality; all the while stripping away decep-tive appearances. As in *Thunder in the Air* or *The Ghost Sonata*, the initial tableau might also serve to mask troubling truths con-cealed behind seemingly tranquil surface appearances. From the patterns of unfolding images and actions there emerge leitmotifs common to all of the Chamber Plays, explored, however, in differ-ent light and mood and with different focus in each. These include the theme of death; either as the process of dying, spiritual pre-paration for death, or death as liberator from suffering in an unclean world. Closely linked to the death theme is that of the material world as an illusion. Ritualised plots of characters unmasking one another and stripping away façades of pretence and deceptive appearances are characteristic of several Chamber Plays. The theme of journeying through life and various stages of death, and of exploring the depths of the psyche, evolve through plots that comprise a series of stage images that convey spatial relationships. In *The Ghost Sonata*, for example, the audience is afforded the point of view of the Student who travels through an apartment house. In the first movement he observes the house façade from the street, while the dialogue revolves around what is seen in the win-dows. The second movement switches perspective and reveals the interior behind the façade, where even the people who live there are forced to shed their appearances through acts of mutual unmasking. The third movement opens up another space deeper inside the building: a beautiful room of a young lady, decorated with hya-cinths, which, as a result of another verbal unmasking, quickly deteriorates and turns into the realm of death.

While the Chamber Plays take place in urban middle-class mili-eus, they abound in servants, maids, and cooks who do not simply belong to the trappings of turn-of-the-century bourgeois house-holds, but play threatening, subversive roles. They are both reminders of social inequity and suggestions of the uneasy incertitude of identity. Perhaps most memorably in *The Ghost Sonata*, a grotesque vampire Cook usurps the members of the family she is supposed to nurture. She feels entitled to suck the blood of the privileged classes, who, for their part, feed on their servants. The vampire Old Man in the same play, who with a chilling gesture draws life-strength from the young Student, is exposed as a former servant of the Colonel's valet; while the Colonel himself is unmasked as a former sponger in other people's kitchens. Society thus appears as a giant roller-coaster of mutual vampirism and cannibalism, enclosed in Strindberg's funhouses where everyone is related to everyone else through deception, adultery, exploitation, enslavement, and through the constant and unpredictable inversion of roles.

This provides an additional leitmotif found in several Chamber Plays, that of vampirism, manifest in the characters' financial, social, emotional, and spiritual usurpation of one another. In *The Pelican* the theme of vampirism takes centre stage, focusing on the figure of the mother who thrives on oppressing her children, so that they would literally starve and freeze to death, were it not for the warmth and consolation they find in the purging flames that ultimately devour them. The title of the play is an ironic image: the pelican, as legend has it, feeds her youngsters with her heart's blood, and in the heraldic tradition it stands as a symbol of the ultimate self-sacrifice of Christ. In the play the figure of the monstrous vampire mother is a tangible oxymoron, just as the vampire cook in *The Ghost Sonata*. For Strindberg, these vampire characters are manifestations of Swedenborg's doctrine of correspondences: symbols of another, terrible reality prevailing beyond our social masks and mundane pretences. Hence also a metatheatrical quality of the Chamber Plays, where life appears as a masquerade and clear vision is afforded only to those wanderers who have had a glimpse of the other side. While working on the new plays, Strindberg was preoccupied with the mythical idea of a 'world weaveress', which he even borrowed as the original title for *The Burned House* (Strindberg 1991: 381–82). In a letter from May 1907 he advises Emil Schering about how to compose drama, echoing his own methods applied in the Chamber Plays: 'Keep to the subject! Don't forget the leitmotiv! Weave people's fates together, the warp and the weft! … A scene = an electric discharge! But charge first, long and well' (Strindberg 1992: 746).

As Strindberg's other works, these too recycle a range of auto-biographical elements, which are crystallised into evocative patterns reminiscent of chamber music. *Thunder in the Air*, for example, exploits Strindberg's anxiety upon Harriet Bosse's intention to re-marry and the perspective of being supplanted in his daughter's life by a stepfather. Bosse, who saw the premiere of the play at the Intimate Theatre, became furious, as Strindberg's defensive letter testifies: 'I warned you not to see it. It is a painful work with which I tried to write you and [our child] out of my heart: I wanted to draw in advance on the anguish I knew I would soon feel' (quoted by Sprinchorn in Strindberg 1962: x). One other instance of utilising autobiographical material in the Chamber Plays can be observed in the setting of *The Burned House*, inspired by the sight of the play-wright's childhood home in ruins. August Falck, the young director of the Intimate Theatre, describes a morning walk on Nortull Street in Stockholm with Strindberg, who caught sight of the remains of the old house that had burned to the ground the previous night:

> We stopped. Strindberg put his hand on my arm and pointed past the yard. In an instant he had seized upon the theatrical effect of an apple tree … that had bloomed under the heat of the fire and stood there like a revelation in the midst of the soot and the homelessness.
>
> (quoted in Lamm 1971: 483)

While Strindberg never hesitated to utilise his life for theatrical purposes, he also warned against all-too-close biographical inter-pretations. Sending the newly completed Chamber Plays to the translator, Schering, he explained:

> Now I beg you, read my new dramas only as that; they are mosaic work as usual, from my own and other people's lives,

but please don't take them as autobiography or confession. Whatever doesn't correspond with the facts, is poetry, not lies.

(Strindberg 1992: 736–37)

As for their contemporary Swedish reception, the Chamber Plays fared even worse than *A Dream Play* or *The Dance of Death*. Intended to create a modern repertoire that would draw audiences to Strindberg's Intimate Theatre, four of the Chamber Plays produced there between 1907 and 1909 could only stay on the programme for very short runs (Strindberg 1966a: 12–13). *The Black Glove* was first produced by Strindberg's daughter, the actress Greta Strindberg von Philp, on her so-called Strindberg Tour in the Swedish provinces in 1910, albeit with little success (Szalczer 2008: 171–73). The Chamber Plays – notably *The Pelican* and *The Ghost Sonata* – achieved great success for the first time in Reinhardt's productions in Germany in the 1910s, and finally became integrated into the Swedish theatre canon from the mid-twentieth century, produced by such great directors as Olof Molander and Ingmar Bergman (see Chapter 13).

10 Modernising history

By the 1870s historical drama, rooted in the traditions of the
Romantic Movement and a patriotic interest in the great heroes of
early Scandinavian history, had become a highly popular form in
the Swedish theatre (Johnson 1963: 18 and Marker and Marker
2002: 2). Strindberg's first produced work, *In Rome* (1870), was a
history play dealing with an episode in the life of the Danish
sculptor Bertel Thorvaldsen. Following the success of this early
experiment – which was given eleven performances at the Royal
Dramatic Theatre – the young Strindberg was ready to burst onto
the national scene with another history play, *Master Olof* (1872).
But it took nine years until the play finally reached the stage in
1881, for, as it turned out, this work challenged all conventions of
the genre. Instead of an idealised hero, *Master Olof* gave Swedish
audiences a complex and dynamic protagonist who resembled all
too closely the defiant young playwright; a rebel who showed signs
of human weakness and internal struggle all too clearly. While the
readers of the Royal Dramatic Theatre rejected the play, arguing
that it 'lacked respect for the sanctity of history' (Lagercrantz 1984:
45), today it is seen as Strindberg's first significant drama and the
first modern Swedish play.

Though Strindberg's history plays are rarely produced outside
Sweden, many of them have become popular works in the playwright's native country and an important part of the theatrical
repertory. That Strindberg wrote a substantial number of history

plays – some twenty (not counting alternate versions of the same play) – warrants their importance for his evolution as a dramatist. He systematically pursued the dramatisation of both Swedish and world history throughout his career, but produced work in the genre most consistently in the early 1900s. After the history plays of his early career his interest in the genre revived in the 1880s, when he wrote two works set in the Middle Ages – *The Secret of the Guild* (1879–80) and *Sir Bengt's Wife* (1882) – as vehicles for his wife Siri. The next upsurge of history plays began with *The Saga of the Folkungs*, *Gustav Vasa*, and *Erik XIV* in 1899 and culminated in 1908 with *The Last Knight*, *The Regent*, and *Earl of Bjälbo*. Over the nine years that these two dates encompass, Strindberg wrote eleven plays dealing with leading figures of Swedish history. With the earlier *Master Olof* added to the series, these plays form a cycle exploring the history of Sweden from the twelfth to the nineteenth century.

In the early 1900s Strindberg became increasingly interested in the relationship between divine providence and the fate of the individual, including that of historical figures. Already his earlier plays on Swedish history present the characters' fates in the light of larger historical patterns. In *Master Olof*, for example, the Swedish religious reformer is shown as an almost unconscious follower of Luther, rather than an original thinker and a conscious rebel. The later plays present Swedish rulers drifting on the currents of world history. In *Gustav III* (1902), for example, reports from the French Revolution serve as the context for both the King's efforts and those of the conspirators against him. The notions of freedom of will versus higher powers, guilt and punishment, pride and atonement are explored in the history plays similarly to the more personally autobiographical pieces of the period, such as the *To Damascus* trilogy (1898, 1901). To illustrate his theory of a transnational and metaphysical 'conscious will' (Strindberg 1996: 219) that shapes the historical process Strindberg started a world-historical cycle about 'The Saga of Humankind' in 1903. Of his grand plan that would encompass all major world-historical events to his day, he completed one play on the German religious reformer Luther, *The Nightingale of Wittenberg*, in 1903, and left behind three shorter pieces from the same year, which focus on the historical periods represented by Moses, Socrates, and Christ, respectively (Johnson 1963: 11–17).

The scope of Strindberg's historical drama and its significance for the Swedish theatre can only be compared to what Shakespeare's histories represent for the English stage. Strindberg's history plays, however, show a great variety in their dramaturgy, focus, language, and mood, so much so, that at first sight one might find little in common in them beside the fact that they feature historical figures (Wirmark 1991: 200–201). The few characteristics they share include the prevalence of biblical allusions, which helped place Swedish history within a wider world-historical and metaphysical context. Moreover, the inescapable presence of the common people – either as a chorus of voices or through individual representatives – colours the power games of monarchs and the upper classes, contributing to what Massimo Ciaravolo has called 'historical polyphony' or even 'cacophony' (Ciaravolo 2009: 177) typical of the dramatist who remained a 'maidservant's son' (see Chapter 1) throughout his career. Thus, starting with *Master Olof* – even before his notorious book *The Swedish People* (1882) in which he challenged the established practice of academic history writing that would construct Swedish history as the history of its kings (see Chapter 1) – Strindberg devised a strategy for a 'democratic revaluation of the past' (Steene 1992: 7). Beyond these recurring patterns, however, the principle that the theme or motif of the play determines the form (Strindberg 1966a: 19) is seen at work in each history play.

That Strindberg's approach to the genre kept changing throughout his career also depended on his constantly shifting worldview under the influence of his readings, personal experience, and the given political climate. The main sources of influence on the earlier history drama included Shakespeare as well as the British cultural historian H. T. Buckle, who viewed human beings as products of their times, in sharp contrast with the idealism and individualism espoused by Romanticism (Palmblad 1927: 26). The history plays of the 1900s, on the other hand, reveal a providential and monistic view of history: a search for a single principle or force underlying the historical process. In his essay 'The Mysticism of World History' (1903) Strindberg views the course of history as a play staged by a higher conscious will:

> as if the world soul had forced its way down into the consciousness of the masses ... [It] is fashioned as an instrument for a will that exists outside us ... , which leads the destinies of peoples and individuals from above.
>
> (Strindberg 1996: 183)

This conception is reminiscent of Hegel's notion of the theatre of world history through which the Spirit strives for an ever-greater consciousness of freedom (Hegel 1988: 12–22). Strindberg's version of the conscious will aims at the unification of humanity, in both a political and a spiritual sense, which can only be accomplished through 'the internal interaction of conflicting forces' (Strindberg 1996: 219), which generates the ups and downs of history, where historical personalities unconsciously play out their roles of alternately uniting or dividing peoples, religions, and cultures. But ultimately, the significance of Strindberg's contributions transcends the range of influences that had shaped his shifting views on the world process, in that his history plays deliberately override and expand generic boundaries in an effort to modernise the genre. What, in the views of contemporary critics, seemed condemnable transgression of the norms – as in the case of *Master Olof*, for example – appears today an ingenious attempt at the revival of the form in ways meaningful to the modern world (Stockenström 1988: 43).

Strindberg's history plays share a number of qualities with the rest of his drama. Through the depth of psychological characterisation (either in the realistic style as in *Master Olof* and *Gustav Vasa* or through a dream-like expressionism as in *Charles XII*), historical personages are shown as modern, shifting, 'characterless characters' similar to those in *Miss Julie* (1888), rather than idealised national heroes. In *Master Olof*, for example, the goal was

> to depict human beings both in their greatness and their triviality; not to avoid the right word; to let history be the

background and to compress historical periods to fit the demands of the [theatre] of our time.

(Strindberg 1966a: 249)

As with the figures of his other plays, Strindberg also imbued his historical characters with elements of self-portrait, showing them entangled both in the domestic problems and in the philosophical dilemmas of his own time. He repeatedly stressed, moreover, the importance of creating 'polyphonic' compositions even in the history plays, where several groups of characters would voice their own truths with equal force, which resulted in a modern dramaturgy undermining the notion of absolute truth. In *Master Olof*, as Strindberg confides to the members of the Intimate Theatre some thirty-five years after the composition of the play:

> I substituted prose for verse, and instead of the opera-like blank verse drama with solo and special numbers, I composed polyphonically, a symphony, in which voices were interwoven (major and minor characters were treated equally), and in which no one accompanied the soloist.
>
> (Strindberg 1966a: 18)

Thus the first major work in which Strindberg both subverted and reinvented the genre was *Master Olof* (1872), about Olaus Petri (1493–1552), the leader of the Lutheran Reformation in Sweden during the reign of Gustav Vasa. *Master Olof* challenges the conventions of history drama particularly because of the modernity of its dialogue and characterisation. Contrary to the expectations of Swedish audiences to see larger-than-life figures declaim elevated verse on stage, the play presents realistic characters portrayed with psychological depth and speaking contemporary colloquial prose. As a major influence Strindberg cites Shakespeare's *Julius Caesar*, a play in which the protagonist is treated as 'merely a human being, and as such, he is almost a minor character in that bit of world history' (Strindberg 1966a: 246). Similarly, Olof is depicted as a person engulfed by the tides of history almost by chance. At the opening of the play he is a young priest, playfully preparing for a recitation with his pupils; he is then gradually coaxed by others into his calling. What points beyond Shakespeare's influence is that Olof is portrayed as a modern, indecisive, and self-conflicted character, shown in moments of self-doubt, and even retracting his views in the face of death. In addition, he is surrounded by strong characters who represent their causes with equal force, including the King, the Catholic Bishop, and Olof's father-in-law, the Anabaptist Gert. Olof's centrality and heroism are undermined as we see him both influenced and used by his opponents. Such presentation of the multiplicity of truth, which underlies the 'polyphonic' structure, presents Olof propelled into action by circumstances, rather than by the conscious choice of a hero.

The twenty-three-year-old dramatist projected his frustration with his time into the figure of Olof, 'the dilemma of the young who wish to revolutionise society and pull down what is old and dead, yet who shrink from violence and violent death', as Michael Meyer observes (1985: 12). This view is supported by journalist Gustaf Uddgren, who became Strindberg's friend in the 1890s and commented that 'All of that generation which was young during the latter part of the seventies ... was carried away by the poet who wrote *Master Olof*' (Uddgren 1920: 13). In the aftermath of the Paris Commune (1871) and its brutal suppression, which affected the rest of Europe, social unrest swept through Sweden in the late 1870s and early 1880s. The play's personal and topical urgency was one of the reasons that, in spite of several revisions, which produced politically tamer versions, including one in verse, *Master Olof* was not produced until 1881. By the time the original prose version finally premiered at the New Theatre in Stockholm, it appeared politically less disturbing and was received favourably as 'a brilliant success' (Strindberg 1992: 50).

Master Olof is the first part of a smaller group of plays, the so-called 'Vasa Trilogy', within the larger Swedish history cycle. In its capacity of dealing with the reign of King Gustav Vasa it is joined by two post-Inferno plays: *Gustav Vasa* (1899) and *Eric XIV* (1899), the latter treating the rule of Gustav's son, Eric. Here again, the motif determining the form of the individual plays is at work (see Strindberg 1966a: 19). *Gustav Vasa* is a realistic presentation of a great ruler and strong central character of mythical proportions, while the weak and 'characterless' Eric is shown as a victim of circumstances. The universe of the former play is ordered by the king's actions and their implications for his nation. The latter work is a character study, where history serves to set the atmosphere and the background for the 'Strindbergian tragic character' similar to Miss Julie (Johnson 1963: 127–28). The fragmentary plot structure reflects Eric's whimsical personality, unable to create anything but a chaotic world around him. Yet, ever since its premiere at the Swedish Theatre in Stockholm in 1899, *Eric XIV* has been one of the favourites of the Swedish public, perhaps because of the main character's psychologically sophisticated, spectacular role (Johnson 1963: 129–30).

Eric XIV was seen in an avant-garde production in 1921 at the Moscow Art Theatre's First Studio, directed by Evgeny Vakhtangov, with Michael Chekhov in the title role. This was the first in a series of productions through which Vakhtangov departed from Stanislavsky's 'lifelike verisimilitude', developing 'a stylised language anti-realistic in form' (Wirmark 1994: 141). For the director, who had embraced the October Revolution, the play carried the 'theme of the doom of an autocratic power' (Rudnitsky 1988: 52–53). Ignaty Nivinsky's expressionistic set represented the royal palace as a prison-like, chaotic, and deathly place at the edge of an abyss. The set featured leaning and bent columns and angular streaks of lightning flickering against a black backdrop. Amidst a 'labyrinth of passages and flights of stairs and landings in the displaced perspective of the broken playing area', Michael Chekhov played Eric

> as a man who has heard the firm, inevitable tread of fate, who knows that his demise is inescapable, and this is why he seems indifferent to everything, apathetic, as if transfixed in his cumbersome silver attire, then suddenly driven into furious activity by terror, the impotence of rage. The tragic was conveyed in the spare, graphically incisive and outwardly cold figure. Abnormally dilating eyes, dropping intonation and the nervous movement of his thin hands betrayed suffering and anguish. At the moment when Eric threw the magnificent royal mantle

from his shoulders with one short, quick movement, his boyish
thinness, his frailty immediately became apparent. Eric personified weakness itself, impotence itself.

(Rudnitsky 1988: 53)

As one critic wrote, it was 'impossible to separate [this production]
from [the] Moscow of the period, from destroyed buildings, red flags,
street posters, Red Army detachments on the march, search-lights
stabbing the night sky above the Kremlin, solitary automobiles
cutting through the streets and rumors flying from flat to flat'
(Rudnitsky 1988: 53).

Several of Strindberg's historical dramas of the 1900s dramatise
the metaphor of *theatrum mundi* (the world as a stage), where
character appears as a set of roles, devoid of an inner self. As
Michael Robinson noted, the 'metatheatrical dimension' of these
plays – their formal construction that draws attention to the world
of the plays as theatre and the characters as actors and marionettes – conveys 'the almost Pirandellian consciousness' (Robinson
1998: 71) of a chilling, modernist sense of inessentiality and alienation. In *Gustav III* (1902) Strindberg found a form through which he
could best present the ruler whom he described as an enlightened
despot 'who carries out the French Revolution at home in Sweden –
that is to say, crushes the aristocrats with the help of the third
estate. ... As a character he is full of contradictions, a tragedian
who plays comedy in life, ... an absolute monarch who is a friend
of liberty, ... the Revolutionist [who] falls at the hand of the
Revolutionists' (Strindberg 1955: 177–78). The play is set in 1789
against the background of the French Revolution and makes use of
the intrigue-ridden, suspenseful, well-made play structure. Gustav,
who was a playwright and is known for his love of the theatre, is
presented as a crowned actor in the play of his nation's history.
He constantly rehearses his role in front of a mirror, wears masks
and costumes and, being aware of his own theatricality, he carefully
plans his entrances and exits. Gustav's rule is a ceremonious performance in the eyes of his subjects; as the aristocrat Fersen remarks
at the court carnival, 'apparently there's a masquerade here the
whole year round' (Strindberg 1955: 260). Behind the scenes the

King plays the role of the conspirator, including the plotting of a *coup d'état*, while he wonders if 'perhaps the whole thing is a play' (Strindberg 1955: 235). But however self-consciously Gustav acts, imagining himself the playwright and the director in control of the stage, on the whole he is a blind tool serving the ends of a higher player. At the end of the play it is the Queen who unknowingly – and as is known, only temporarily – saves him from assassination, and as they are reconciled, he declares that 'the queen is the strongest piece in the game and has the function of protecting the king' (Strindberg 1955: 265). *Gustav III* illustrates most clearly Strindberg's view of history in 'The Mysticism of World History', as 'an enormous game of chess played by a single player who moves both black and white, is completely impartial … , is for himself and against himself, … and has only one aim: to maintain balance and justice while ending the match in a draw' (Strindberg 1996: 191).

The heroine of *Queen Christina* (1901) is the Swedish monarch known for her love of art and learning (for example, she famously invited the French philosopher Descartes to stay at her court); for her conversion to Catholicism in Protestant Sweden even though it meant her political suicide; and for her abdication in 1654. In the play she is portrayed as an elusive character, appearing in a different role for each of her subjects. As parallels with the fictitious Miss Julie reveal, Christina must have been an intriguing figure for Strindberg. According to the testimony of both historical records and anecdotal sources, she was brought up as a boy, educated as a prince, and at her coronation at age six took an oath as king rather than queen. Strindberg thought of Christina as a 'woman hater' and a woman 'fighting for her self-existence, against her feminine nature' (Strindberg 1955: 3), and portrayed her as a self-conflicted character escaping from her responsibilities into role-playing. The play concludes with a private masque of the Greek Pandora myth, which Christina stages for her lover Claes Tott; a performance that turns into a political confrontation and the Queen's awakening to the dire reality of her mistreated people and country. As Christina enacts the first woman, created by Zeus in order to release from her box all troubles and evils on earth, the curtain in the palace chamber falls to reveal a tableau of strangers: the people suffering under her careless rule. Crushed and humiliated, she then announces her abdication and her wish to freely return to the faith of her forefathers. From a feminist perspective, in Margareta Fahlgren's assessment, the play presents a female ruler trapped by a patriarchal gender structure where the final sequence shows the marginalisation of femininity. The public woman situated in the centre of power must be eliminated so that she ceases to be a threat to the patriarchal order. Expelled from the power-centre, she is then resurrected as a private woman submitting to male authority, represented by her dead father Gustav Adolf (Fahlgren 1994a: 89–91).

Charles XII (1901) is an example of yet another form: the expressionistic dream play with a historical theme. It focuses on the last few years, 1715–18, of the reign of the celebrated warrior king, whose irresponsible military campaigns, Strindberg felt, had destroyed Sweden. But far from being a political intrigue play, as exemplified by *Gustav III*, *Charles XII* is a contemplative piece with a completely inactive protagonist preparing for death. Throughout the play Charles remains passive and reclusive, while other characters refer to him as a shadow and a living dead. The plot consists of a series of tableaux where the king's internal struggle, the ruinous consequences of his past actions, and his victims both dead and alive, appear in visions, dreams, and hallucinations. Strindberg applies the technique he developed in *To Damascus* I (1898) to create a sense of half-reality: musical and visual leitmotifs (a melancholy saraband by Bach and the image of fire) accentuate subtle transitions between dream and reality, the external and the internal, the material and the spiritual.

Spanning Strindberg's entire career, the history plays encompass a great variety of styles and approaches and are integral to the dramatist's endeavour to modernise the theatre. In 1998 a monumental production based on his Vasa-dynasty plays, entitled *Vasasagan*, was mounted by director Staffan Valdemar Holm with scenographer Bente Lykke Møller at the Dramatic Theatre in Malmö, Sweden. The production included scenes from *The Last Knight* (1908), *The Regent* (1908), *Master Olof* (1872), *Gustav Vasa* (1899), *Eric XIV* (1899), *Gustav Adolf* (1900), and *Queen Christina* (1901), arranged in historically chronological order, dealing with the period

Figure 4 Nina Togner-Fex and Hans Peter Edh in the *Queen Christina* sequence of *Vasasagan*, directed by Staffan Waldemar Holm, Malmö City Theatre, 1998. Photo by Anders Mattsson, courtesy of Malmö Stadsteater.

1520–1654. Holm and Møller have become known for their provocative reassessments of the classics. In their productions they strip away petrified layers of traditional interpretations and performance conventions, and foreground presentational, non-psychological, and visual production elements (see Chapter 11 on their 1992 production of *Miss Julie*). For *Vasasagan*, dramaturgs Karen-Maria Bille and Stellan Larsson created a three-part performance script, based on the text of Strindberg's seven history plays, which comprised a prologue and thirty-three scenes, and took approximately six hours to perform. The performance was staged in a minimalist set where flexible space was created by three mobile walls on wheels, changing positions to construct a new space for each scene. Against this simple and timeless background the performers appeared in lavish

costumes, performing stylised, often ritualised actions while incorporating a wide range of traditional performance styles such as
'tableaux vivants, pantomime, pageant wagons and the carnival
tradition' (Smidig 2006: 236). While Strindberg's drama, including
the history plays, can be seen on the whole as a modernist cultural
critique and revaluation of the theatre, Holm's production emerged
as a post-modern commentary on the construction and mechanisms
of power and on the construction and mechanisms of the theatre
itself.

PART IV

Key plays/productions

Miss Julie (1888), *A Dream Play* (1901), and *The Ghost Sonata* (1907) are among Strindberg's best known and internationally most often produced plays. Each represents a different creative outlook and offers a radically innovative dramaturgy (see Part III). While at the time of their first appearance these plays were considered utterly controversial – either for political reasons as in the case of *Miss Julie* (see Chapter 3), or, as we shall see, because they were deemed impossible to stage – they came to exert a lasting influence on the theatre and have inspired directors, designers, performers, and playwrights worldwide. A survey of some key productions of these plays reveals how changing historical contexts have moulded their meanings, stagings, and reception.

11 *Miss Julie*
From failed world premiere to worldwide acclaim

The world premiere of *Miss Julie* was planned for March 1889 at the Dagmar Theatre in Copenhagen, Denmark, as part of the inaugural programme of the Scandinavian Experimental Theatre founded by Strindberg and his wife Siri von Essen (see Chapter 3). But on the day of the dress rehearsal the play was banned from public performance – on the grounds of indecency – by the Danish Ministry of Justice, and it was not to be seen on the professional stages of Scandinavia until 1906. Instead, the world premiere took place at a private performance in a shabby hall of the Student Union of the University of Copenhagen on 14 March 1889, followed by a second performance the next day, completing the short history of the Scandinavian Experimental Theatre. Since the company had no stage director, Siri as artistic director and Strindberg as the playwright were responsible for the staging. Some 150, overwhelmingly male, audience members were crowded in the small room, and in spite of the makeshift stage, reviews described the set as surprisingly faithful to the stage directions, with real kitchen utensils and a large stove. The ballet sequence was cut, and only a tune played on a flute could be heard as Jean and Julie briefly retired from the kitchen. Siri, who had been absent from the stage since the early 1880s, created an 'all too cold' Miss Julie to appear seductive. Viggo Schiwe's Jean was criticised as too 'gentlemanlike' to be convincing as a servant. Only Henriette Pio was praised as a perfect Christine. In spite of the poor resources and a weak cast, critics were taken by the powerful dramatic effect of the piece (Ollén 1961: 135–36).

Following the controversies of its initial reception *Miss Julie* was produced successfully for the first time at the Théâtre-Libre in Paris in 1893 (see Chapter 4). The play finally came to enjoy worldwide popularity in the twentieth century as the frequency of its stage productions steadily increased from the 1920s in countries ranging from New Zealand, China, Japan, Mexico, and Argentina to Russia and the United States. Besides stage interpretations, the play inspired many transpositions into other media, including film, opera, musical, radio, television, and ballet (see Törnqvist and Jacobs 1988: 148–270). The earliest, now lost, silent film adaptation was directed by the Swedish filmmaker Anna Hofman-Uddgren in 1912, starring members of the original Intimate Theatre (see Chapter 6), Manda Björling as Julie and August Falck as Jean. Another influential cinematic rendition was German director Felix Basch's 1921 silent motion picture with Asta Nielsen as Julie. Swedish choreographer Birgit Cullberg's 1950 ballet version with music by Ture Rangström has often been revived on the stage and was made into a television production in 1981. From these countless versions the

Figure 5 Manda Björling, Sacha Sjöström, and August Falck in *Miss Julie*, Folkteatern, Stockholm, directed by August Falck in 1906. Courtesy of the Strindberg Museum, Stockholm, Sweden.

following overview samples some important productions that help to trace how this remarkable play came to participate, through performance, in diverse cultural and political discourses over the span of a century.

Breakthrough in Sweden: August Falck's *Miss Julie*, 1906

The Swedish public saw *Miss Julie* for the first time in 1906, nearly two decades after its completion, at the locale of the Academic Union of Lund. It was the newly created company of twenty-four-year-old actor-manager August Falck that ventured to present the play, which had been declared indecent and morally dangerous, in the dramatist's homeland. As one reviewer remarked, the reason for such a late arrival was that Swedish theatres rejected the piece because it proposed to reform the theatre. Falck directed the production with Manda Björling as 'an elegant Julie' (Ollén 1961: 138), August Palme as Jean and Sacha Sjöström as Christine. Still in the same year, the production moved to Folkteatern in Stockholm, this time with Falck playing Jean. Reviewers praised the 'brave little trio from the provinces' that dared what well-established Stockholm theatre owners shied away from.[1] The performers were generally applauded, though Björling was not considered convincing as a seductress. She was nevertheless praised for portraying Julie's 'anxiety and the despair of deep inner strife' with shocking truthfulness. Falck's Jean at first seemed to critics too much of a man of the world for a lackey, but when he 'felt himself superior [to Julie] and grasped the power to avenge and oppress, he found the right tone'.[2] One review noted that despite low expectations – after all 'Mr. August Falck's company is very new ... [and] young and untested. And can anything good come from the provinces?' – audiences were in for a pleasant surprise which proved that 'good plays make good actors' and that 'Strindberg's plays must be seen, not read'.[3]

The triumph of *Miss Julie* in Stockholm culminated in the creation of the Intimate Theatre by Falck and Strindberg in 1907 (see Chapter 6), which continued to perform the play as one of its most successful productions. At this stage of his career, however, Strindberg warned the company against a naturalistic setting, even though he

found it understandable that the young director was influenced by
the Preface of *Miss Julie*, which 'recommended that one try to
achieve reality. ... Falck, faithful to the program, had [as his set] a
kitchen complete in all details'. But, Strindberg adds in *Open letters
to the Intimate Theatre*, 'I wrote that twenty years ago' (Strindberg
1966a: 296). While the dramatist felt that the play was still meaningful for a modern public in 1906, he recognised that its presentation needed to adjust to the demands of the changing times. These
new demands, he felt, would be best served by a subdued, poetic,
and simplified staging, rather than by a painstaking realism.

Modernist giants of the Swedish stage

Alf Sjöberg: Miss Julie *in Stockholm (1949) and on the screen (1951)*

A new milestone in the production history of *Miss Julie* came about
with Alf Sjöberg's (1903–80) staging in 1949 – for the centennial
celebrations of Strindberg's birth – at the Royal Dramatic Theatre,
popularly called Dramaten, in Stockholm. The action was placed in
a carefully elaborated psychological setting, which consisted of 'a
cave-like room where the characters move[d] around, like prisoners
between two clearly separated play areas, indicated by lighting'.
As a visual suggestion of even darker inner realms, spectators could
see into Jean's trap-like room with its 'brutally laid bed' (quoted in
Törnqvist and Jacobs 1988: 244–45). The naturalistic emphasis on
external detail was replaced by an expressionistic approach to the
physical environment, which clearly reflected the characters' unconscious. As one reviewer remarked, 'Sjöberg made the stage business
around the Count's speaking tube into a sort of expressionistic
dread-effect'.[4] Others noted the intense Midsummer mood which
could even be smelled as the kitchen steam and the fragrance of
lilacs blended in the stifling air. In the final scene Julie appeared in a
black travelling cape, suggestive of her 'last journey', and at
the moment of Jean's final speech, ordering her to leave with razor in
hand, her black figure was seen against 'the open door (freedom)
and the light exterior with its raising sun (of grace), while Jean
remained in the dark interior' (Törnqvist and Jacobs 1988: 161).

Figure 6 Inga Tidblad and Ulf Palme in *Miss Julie* at The Royal Dramatic
Theatre, Stockholm, directed by Alf Sjöberg, 1949. Photo by Sven
Järlås, courtesy of The Royal Dramatic Theatre.

Inga Tidblad's Julie had a riveting effect on viewers, as her performance
included 'all the complexities that Strindberg put in this character'.
Ulf Palme's Jean was characterised as 'perfect' and 'indescribable' and
Märta Dorff was praised as an excellent Christine.[5] The director
attributed the success of the production to a special rehearsal strategy:

> From a work-hypothetical point of view, we regarded the play
> as presented by two voices – within one and the same person.
> We called them ... the male and the female voice. The male
> voice was hard and repressive, annihilating and victorious. The
> female voice was the voice of sensitivity, submission, humility.
> These two voices were addressing one another. What was
> interesting and exciting to us was that these disputing demons
> sometimes lent their voices to Jean, sometimes to Julie. The
> two voices passed through the two, left one of them for
> the other. It was a strange meeting which was at the same time

separation. Jean and Julie seemed to change roles, minds, their limits flowed over in one another.

> (Sjöberg 1982: 227, quoted in Törnqvist and
> Jacobs 1988: 245)

While Sjöberg clearly associated traditional gender roles with stereotypical male and female behaviour, his dynamic approach to character helped the actors to create a psychological complexity that Strindberg suggested by the unconventional handling of dialogue described in his Preface to *Miss Julie* (see Chapter 7).

Sjöberg's 1951 film version – which won a shared first prize at the Cannes Film Festival the same year – offers yet another approach to the play while taking full advantage of cinematic devices. Strindberg's condensed 'slice of life' is replaced in the film by a dream-like narrative in which the same story is shown from several shifting perspectives, including that of Julie (Anita Björck) and Jean (Ulf Palme). Strindberg's sparse setting that concentrates the action at one place – the Count's kitchen – is eliminated, and the story unfolds at various interior and exterior locations, while visual metaphors take over the primary role of the dialogue. The dreams and childhood stories which Julie and Jean tell each other are visualised in a series of extended flashbacks. Consequently, the intimate, three-character drama is conveyed by a profusion of characters, in which the emphasis switches from Julie and Jean's relationship in the present to the love–hate struggle between Julie's father and mother in the past, in the shadow of the portraits of all of her ancestors. The cinematic version shifts all guilt for Julie's destruction onto her vengeful, plebeian mother, thereby reinstating the stereotypical gender divide that Sjöberg's own stage version, as well as Strindberg's play, had transgressed.

Ingmar Bergman: Miss Julie *in Munich (1981) and in Stockholm (1985)*

Acclaimed Swedish filmmaker and stage director Ingmar Bergman (1918–2007) staged two remarkable productions of *Miss Julie* in the 1980s. During the late 1970s and early 1980s he worked as a director at the Residenztheater in Munich, Germany (Steene 2005: 45). In 1981 he directed there what was nicknamed 'The Bergman Project':

a simultaneous production of three plays that dealt with the effect of society upon the relationship between the sexes. The plays included *Nora*, Bergman's adaptation of Ibsen's *A Doll's House*; *Julie*, his version of *Miss Julie*; and the stage adaptation of his own film *Scenes from a Marriage* (see Marker and Marker 1999). The characteristically 'Bergmanesque' interpretation of *Julie*, in Peter Weiss's German translation, stemmed from a few alterations in Strindberg's text. Namely, Bergman restored a line which he found in the original manuscript but which was deleted from later versions (Marker and Marker 1999: 15). Jean relates to Christine how he saw Miss Julie train her fiancé to jump over her riding crop, until the young man grabbed the crop and struck her on the face with it. In the published text Strindberg eliminated the slap and instead had the fiancé throw the crop on the ground and leave. Bergman based his entire interpretation on the missing line, which he construed as Strindberg's 'original' intention: his Julie had a scar on her face – caused by the slap – which she was desperately trying to hide under thick white make-up. Thus Bergman's Julie (Anne-Marie Kuster) was wounded from the outset, both physically and psychologically, which made her an easy prey for the robust Jean (Michael Degen) and Christine (Gundi Ellert). Her mask – created by the thick make-up – which could hardly conceal her vulnerability, came off altogether after her intercourse with Jean. As she re-emerged from his room, her scar was bleeding as a visible sign of her death throes. That at the end Julie still came off as the strongest character, who consciously chose death over dishonour, depended on another textual change: Bergman's cut of the hypnosis scene (Marker and Marker 1999: 14, 32–33). Rather than begging Jean to hypnotise her into suicide, Bergman's Julie simply picked up Jean's razor from the table and ascended the steps that led out of the kitchen, leaving a cowardly, servile Jean behind.

Having returned to Stockholm, Bergman staged *Miss Julie* again at Dramaten in 1985. In many respects the production was similar to his Munich *Julie*, but the play was now performed on its own and on a small stage. Gunilla Palmstierna-Weiss's set design showed the kitchen level where a large beam suggested a towering super-structure, the world of the Count, above. In this production Bergman

Figure 7 Marie Göranzon and Peter Stormare in *Miss Julie* at The Royal Dramatic Theatre, Stockholm, directed by Ingmar Bergman, 1985. Photo by Bengt Wanselius, courtesy of The Royal Dramatic Theatre.

kept Julie's (Marie Göranzon, in later revivals Lena Olin) scar but did not stress the blood symbolism. Here too, as in the previous production, there was a young, strong, and sensual Christine (Gerti Kulle) who ruled not only in the kitchen but also over Jean (Peter Stormare). Strindberg's 'ballet' was developed into an elaborate interlude. As Julie and Jean retired into the latter's room, the kitchen was invaded by a group of peasants who enacted a sexually explicit drunken orgy. The hierarchical relationships and sexual liaisons among the peasants reflected the power struggles acted out by Miss Julie, Jean, and Christine (Törnqvist and Jacobs 1988: 173–76). In Bergman's staging Christine was awakened by the noise, came into the kitchen and chased out the fornicating peasants. She then remained there seated but unseen by Julie as the latter entered, deathly pale, from Jean's room and ran outside to vomit. Only then did Christine withdraw again into her room, fully aware of what had taken place between her mistress and her fiancé.

In the Stockholm version Bergman replaced the hypnosis scene with physical action. Standing close behind Miss Julie, Jean held up a hand-mirror so that she could see herself putting the razor to her own throat, as if rehearsing her suicide. Like a dark shadow, Jean's figure merged with Julie's, but at the same time he turned his face away and assumed a servile position. Julie, on the other hand, looked straight into the mirror, facing herself and her future with dignity. She then did not even notice as Jean ran into his room and came back with the money that she had stolen from her father, stuffing the banknotes into her dress pocket so as to erase any trace of his involvement. After Miss Julie ascended the kitchen stairs and vanished into the sunlight, Jean took out her bird-cage from the kitchen, only to return and go on with his normal chores as if nothing had happened (Törnqvist and Jacobs 1988: 180–81, 183).

Miss Julie as political theatre

Rainer Werner Fassbinder, Frankfurt, 1974

In 1974 *Fräulein Julie* was staged in Frankfurt, the Federal Republic of Germany, at the Theater am Turm (TAT), with Rainer Werner

Fassbinder (1945–82) in the role of Jean. Fassbinder, an internationally renowned figure of post-Second World War German anti-
establishment cinema, had worked in the theatre as a director,
actor, and playwright since the early 1960s, first as a member of the
so-called Munich *action-theater*, and since 1968 as a leader of
the so-called '*antiteater*' group (see Barnett 2005: 12–119). At the
time of the Strindberg production, Fassbinder had been recently
appointed artistic director of the TAT, which comprised several
lead actors in his films, including Margit Carstensen who played
Julie and Irm Hermann who created Christine. At this time the
TAT was experimenting with '*Mitbestimmung*' or collective decision making, a new organisational structure that emerged in the
West German theatre in 1969 as an alternative to the autocratic
leadership and hierarchical bureaucracy of the state theatre system
(Barnett 2005: 175–76).

This experiment with a more democratic company structure
provides the background for the rehearsal process of *Miss Julie*,
fraught with complex company politics. In his recent book on
Fassbinder's theatre David Barnett examines documents that shed
light on the controversies surrounding the production. Television
director Ula Stöckl was contracted to direct the piece. Records
reveal, however, that company members felt she had difficulties
with the text and was indecisive in her interpretation. For example,
turning back in time to the Romantic tradition, she perceived Julie's
suicide as a proof of love, with the result that Fassbinder, an artist
known for his political radicalism, threatened to quit his role as
Jean. In addition, the director found it troublesome to direct
Carstensen, who had been accustomed to Fassbinder's demand for
stylised acting in his highly theatricalised films. When the introduction of a second director from the company to assist Stöckl only
worsened the situation, Fassbinder decided to cancel the production,
but the company voted against his decision. Finally, Fassbinder took
over the direction and the production opened with only a week's
delay, on 13 October, as a scorching critique of contemporary
class-society (Barnett 2005: 202–3).

There was no trace of naturalism in any aspect of the performance. The set was sparse and highly symbolic; it consisted of a

Figure 8 Rainer Werner Fassbinder and Margit Carstensen in *Fräulein Julie* (*Miss Julie*), directed by Fassbinder, Ula Stöckl and the company, Theater am Turm, Frankfurt am Main, 1974. Courtesy of the Rainer Werner Fassbinder Foundation.

completely white stage, 'dazzling the audience with an air of unreality' (Barnett 2005: 203), which was 'broken only by a large staircase'[6] that connected the kitchen in the basement with the upper regions of the building that remained invisible. This flight of white stairs compellingly signified Julie's and Jean's struggles towards an unattainable identity which they respectively dreamed of. Their 'inability to escape was made clear ... when they started to make the climb [on the stairs] but had to turn back' (Barnett 2005: 203). The bright lights of the set in the sterile environment made one critic feel that the audience was 'in a dissecting room watching the interaction of human subjects' (Barnett 2005: 205).

Several reviewers noted that the Julie of this production was doomed from the start and the acting made it clear that she had no chance to survive (see Barnett 2005: 205). 'As soon as Carstensen enters for the first time ... the audience understands that Julie has a rendezvous with death.'[7] The boldness of the interpretation culminated in the scene where Julie – according to the script – declared she wanted nothing more than to drink blood from Jean's skull and see his brain on the chopping block. These lines, which are traditionally understood as an expression of her contempt for Jean and the entire male sex, were uttered here as if in a state of rapture, punctuating 'a tender love scene where [Julie and Jean] embrace[d] each other, and the most violent abuses turn[ed] into a confidential love declaration'.[8] The unorthodox interpretation of this scene fit into the 'thesis' Fassbinder had espoused in his films, namely that 'love in a class-society may easily degenerate into sadomasochistic and vampiristic forms'.[9]

The acting in this production seemed 'cool' and detached, only Christine was allowed 'an emotional outburst' (Barnett 2005: 205). Fassbinder was praised as an original actor who presented his role stylised, with a series of clearly marked gestures. His acting was seen as dialectical and Brechtian in that he was both distanced from and close to his character, emotionally alienating spectators while at the same time inviting them to identify.[10] The production was also contextualised by critics in terms of Strindberg's influence on Fassbinder's cinema, making specific comparisons between *Miss Julie* and such films as *The Bitter Tears of Petra von Kant* (1972) and *Fear of Fear* (1975), in which women trapped in a claustrophobic, indifferent, and avaricious society, struggle to come to terms with questions of identity.[11] Both Miss Julie and Petra von Kant rebel against societal rules, while *Fear of Fear* focuses on a woman who is, like Julie, in 'profound conflict with herself'. Like

Strindberg, Fassbinder was interested in the complex interrelation-
ships between the personal and the political and his films reveal the
profound influence of Strindberg's 'combination of psychology,
naturalism, and boldly concentrated style, which paved the way for
expressionism'.[12]

Miss Julie *as anti-apartheid performance:*
Cape Town, 1985

In 1985 a remarkable *Miss Julie* was staged by director Bobby
Heaney at the Baxter Theatre Centre in Cape Town, South Africa.
This performing arts complex, which today offers some one thousand performances annually, opened in 1977 on the premises of the
University of Cape Town. From its inception, the Baxter Theatre's
mission has been to reflect the cultures of all the people of South
Africa,[13] a daring undertaking under apartheid, where segregation
was the norm in all areas of public and private life, including the
theatre. However, because of the protection of academic freedom
that extended to the theatre located on university premises, the
Baxter could avoid the stifling government control that most
theatres were subject to. The multi-racial cast included Sandra
Prinsloo, one of South Africa's most popular actresses, as Julie;
playwright, actor, director John Kani as Jean; and Natie Rula as
Christine.

   In apartheid South Africa the class conflict of the play was
articulated in terms of race. One of the most infamous laws of
South Africa, the Immorality Act of 1950, had declared interracial
sexual relations a criminal offence. Critic Stephen Gray wrote of the
circumstances of the production:

> This year the Immorality Act came up for Parliamentary
> review. Somewhat exploitatively, but nevertheless relevantly,
> the Baxter lauched [*sic*] a production of Strindberg's *Miss Julie*
> of 1888, initially banned for years in Scandinavia for its endor-
> sement of improper class conduct. In South Africa, class equals
> race (at least in the public mind), and here Miss Julie was
> played by the darling of the whites, Sandra Prinsloo, and her

servant by the leading man of South African theatre, John Kani.
As the Immorality Act was scrapped at one end of town, so the
play stirred a furore of backlash from the right-wing lunatic
fringe at the other – bomb threats, ... protests. And yes, circumstances have changed in South African theatre. The production was not banned; indeed, the performers now played
under police protection.

(Gray 1985: 12)

Thus adapted to the specific political situation, the incendiary force
of the nearly hundred-year-old play was revealed once again, as
the performance still provoked outrage and rioting among audience
members. Several sources recall the on-stage kissing between the
white Julie and her black servant, shocking white spectators, who
left in protest in the middle of the performance.[14] In his book on
South Africa's political history G. Leach comments a year after the
premiere:

The theory of separation, in its ultimate form, decreed that
even sex between the races should be prohibited. ... One can
imagine the outrage ... when one of South Africa's best known
Afrikaner [white] actresses, Sandra Prinsloo, appeared on stage
with black actor John Kani in a production of Strindberg's
Miss Julie, the study of a master–servant relationship which
was adapted to South Africa's racial situation. Miss Prinsloo,
who was seen on stage in a stylized seduction of her black
co-star, received several threatening telephone calls, one caller
saying: 'How dare you, Afrikaner daughter'.

(Leach 1986: 36–37)

Another critic marvelled, 'this has never happened before, that a
black and a white person kiss one another on the stage, i.e. pub-
licly. ... And no censorship!'[15] Despite the more lax legislation,
both Prinsloo and Kani received a host of hate mail and death
threats after opening night. Regardless the police protection, John
Kani wound up in hospital with several stab wounds, according
to his online biography.[16] Moreover, Julie's suicide 'was seen

[by white spectators] as the only way out of the humiliation, which had arisen because she had trespassed racial law. The moral of the play to the audience became: look, this is what happens to white women who have intimate relations with black men.'[17]

A production photograph that captures the moment right before Miss Julie's pet bird is beheaded by Jean shows Prinsloo as Julie playing with a live white dove, oblivious of the dark future awaiting her. The use of a dove as a symbol of peace, rather than the siskin specified by Strindberg, was a significant directorial choice in South Africa before the end of apartheid. This production of *Miss Julie* then played an important role in the democratisation of South African theatre, and, as Stephen Gray wrote in 1985, it can be seen

Figure 9 Sandra Prinsloo and John Kani in *Miss Julie* at the Baxter Theatre, Cape Town, South Africa, directed by Bobby Heaney, 1985. Photo by Alex 'Tug' Wilson (touring at the Royal Lyceum Theatre in Edinburgh, 1985). Courtesy of the Baxter Theatre Centre.

as part of the process of 'learning to use the language everyone in that mixed auditorium understands. And learning to know that in the end it is not significant whether a cast is racially mixed or not, that everyone is free to play any role, without reference to creed or colour' (Gray 1985: 17).

Post-modern *Miss Julie*

The New Scandinavian Experimental Theatre: Miss Julie *in Copenhagen, 1992*

By all accounts an unconventional production, *Miss Julie* was staged in 1992 at the New Scandinavian Experimental Theatre in Copenhagen: a group of young directors, designers, and performers who considered themselves heirs of Strindberg's own theatre in the same city, founded in 1888 (see Chapter 3). The production, which won the Danish Critics' Prize, was directed by Staffan Waldemar Holm, who in his programme note explained that he had deliberately broken away from the canonical realistic-psychological approach to the play in order to emphasise its ritualistic aspects: both the sexual ritual and the ritual of death (Sauter et al. 1993: 4–6). According to the director, what made *Miss Julie* relevant to a young audience of 1992 was not the characters' psychological make-up, but the play's inherent raw eroticism. Holm's staging included a series of swiftly unfolding sequences of choreographed copulation, masturbation, and sexual violence, administered with a complete lack of emotion on the characters' part (Lide 1998: 85).

Against the background of a white-tiled wall in a literally empty space, designed by Bente Lykke Møller, the play's class and gender battles, along with its naturalistic rhetoric, were deconstructed in a stylised ritual. The sterile-looking rectangular box connoted as much a public toilet or a slaughterhouse as a generic kitchen (Sauter et al. 1993: 6–7). Møller's cartoonish costumes stressed the cliché aspects of the characters: a Barbie-like Miss Julie (Berrit Kvorning) wore a long silk dress, high heels, and blonde curly locks, while Jean (Henrik Jandorf), in all black, paraded in a beret, a tight seaman's jumper, black pants, and boots. Christine (Bodil Larssen) was dressed like an innocent-looking little girl, in a skirt with suspenders, a blouse with puffy sleeves, and an enormous bow in her hair. Her first appearance set the tone for the performance: with a roguish expression on her face she stood alone in front of the coldly lit, white-tiled wall and made a few dance steps to a well-known Swedish Midsummer melody, while mixing the abortive for Miss Julie's dog in a bowl. Introducing the keynote of the production, the Count's boots followed her, floating in the air, preceding Jean's entrance (Lide 1998: 86).[18]

The performance consisted of a pastiche of farce, melodrama, burlesque, and contemporary pop culture, including borrowings from the video performances of such popular media personalities as Madonna. When, for example, Christine, according to Strindberg's text, would emerge from her room dressed for church, Larssen simply took off her blouse and stood there topless, so that her nipples were covered only by the suspenders, alluding to a well-known Madonna video. Jean's line – 'Dressed for church, already?' – created a comic contrast between the character's physical appearance and the dialogue, a typical technique throughout the production (Lide 1998: 88).

The scenes of what one critic called 'pornographic highlights' were accompanied by Swedish folk music and voodoo drumming that enhanced the ritualistic quality of such stage business as Jean licking Julie's shoes or taking her from behind, to the feigned surprise of Christine, who, in turn, also 'enjoy[ed] moments of mastery over Julie … [for example when] forcing her into a servile position' (Sauter et al. 1993: 9). The absent Count – through the vicarious presence of his boots, used as sex-toys – also partook in the erotic power-game, when, for instance, Jean made love to Christine sticking one boot under her skirt until she reached orgasm (Lide 1998: 86). The conflation of sex and death was sealed as Julie licked the razorblade before her final exit, while Jean triumphantly masturbated.[19]

The advanced physical technique of the performers when carrying out choreographed movements with utmost precision yet cartoonish lightness prevented spectators from empathising with individual characters. In Holm's anti-psychological staging spectators were given the role of voyeurs in a peep-show where 'everyone [was] really getting what he/she want[ed]' (Sauter et al. 1993: 9), thus surreptitiously being made part of a power game of domination and submission, desire and fetish creation. Removed from its traditional context, the *Miss Julie* of this production ultimately became a provocative commentary on contemporary hegemonic media culture.

Anne Bogart's Miss Julie, *Louisville, USA, 1997*

In her 1997 production at the Actors Theatre of Louisville, American director Anne Bogart staged the sexual and class strife between Julie and Jean in a space that connoted 'a wrestling ring or a videogame or the arena for an exploitation TV show like "American Gladiators"'.[20] Paul Owen's 'wildly contemporary' set[21] consisted of a red chequered playing area surrounded by a railing, where the characters and props popped up through traps in the floor from the 'underground' where the servants' quarters were located. As spectators arrived, Christine (Kelly Maurer) was seen alone on the stage mechanically carrying out routine chores for an extended period of time (Frye 1997: 532). Following this pre-show sequence the main contesters entered to ear-splitting rock music: Jean (Jefferson Mays) popped up through the stage floor, and Julie (Ellen Lauren), having entered through the auditorium, climbed over the railing surrounding the stage. The action took place within a 'boxing ring' in a stylised, acrobatic manner, accompanied by the cheers and whistles of scantily dressed cast members from the sides. Julie's stepping down to the lower class was visualised as her descent into the 'underworld' through a trap-door in the floor.

The main action was divided into segments, each ending with what Brecht called a 'social *gest*': a physical metaphor of the power relations that had just been enacted. Such bits of stage business as 'the tossing down of the handkerchief; the drinking of the beer; and the kissing of Julie's foot' (Frye 1997: 534) marked climactic instances in the plot, indicating successive stages of seduction/domination between Julie and Jean. During their off-stage intercourse, these gestures were repeated in a frenzied, sexually explicit dance by the chorus of servants on stage while Christine walked about among them, sipping tea.[22] As the Count's bell rang sharply at the conclusion of the game, Jean, like Pavlov's dog, leaped onto the table, ready 'to answer his master's call' (Frye 1997: 534).

Notes

1 E. N—m, 'En Strindbergspremiär i Stockholm', *Dagens Nyheter*, 14 December 1906.

2 Ibid.

3 A. B—s., 'Folkteatern: "Fröken Julie"', *Svenska Dagbladet*, 11 December 1906.

4 *Social-Demokraten*, 24 January 1949.

5 Ivar Harrie, *Expressen*, 24 January 1949.

6 Chr Braad Thomsen. 'Fassbinders Julie', *Sydsvenska Dagbladet*, 8 April 1975.

7 Ibid.

8 Ibid.

9 Ibid.

10 Ibid.

11 Eva Engström. 'Fassbinder spelar Strindbergs Jean på egna teater', *Dagens Nyheter*, 16 October 1974.

12 http://jclarkmedia.com/fassbinder/fassbinder25.html (accessed 20 November 2007).

13 See *The Baxter Theatre Annual Review* 2007; www.baxter.co.za/review2007.pdf (accessed 7 October 2008).

14 See also 'Baxter Theatre 30th Anniversary Retrospective', *The Mail & Guardian*, 24 August 2007; www.christhurman.net/reviews-interviews/baxter-theatre-30th-anniversary-retrospective.html (accessed 7 October 2008).

15 Arnold Blumer, *Theater Heute* (June 1985): 61, quoted in Törnqvist and Jacobs 1988: 259.

16 'Dr. John Kani', in 'Who's Who of Southern Africa'; www.whoswhosa.co.za/Pages/profilefull.aspx?IndID=3081 (accessed 7 October 2008).

17 Blumer, quoted in Törnqvist and Jacobs 1988: 260.

18 See also Larsolof Carlsson, 'Fräkt grepp på fröken Julie', *Helsingborgs Dagblad*, 5 March 1992.

19 Ibid.

20 Chris Jones, '*Miss Julie*', *Variety*, 2 February 1997. www.variety.com/index.asp?layout=print_review&reviewid=VE1117432697& categoryid=33 (accessed 20 October 2008).

21 Ibid.

22 Ibid.

12 *A Dream Play*
From closet drama to post-modern performance

For many years following its publication in 1902 *A Dream Play* was
considered a reading drama that lacked dramatic action and presented instead 'the spooky, contourless life of dreams', which was
great poetry but alien to the theatre (Bark 1981: 84). It was a play
unlike anything that had been produced on the Swedish stage
before. Even in the larger context of the European theatre the play
was much ahead of its time and constituted a unique challenge to
existing stagecraft. When in 1907 director Victor Castegren per-
suaded Albert Ranft, the owner of The Swedish Theatre (Svenska
Teatern) in Stockholm, to put on the play, there were seemingly
insurmountable difficulties to overcome. These included the challenge of creating a dream atmosphere on stage. The script itself
offers strategies for visual transformations without heavy machinery
and too many set changes. Shifts in location are suggested in the
stage directions, for example, by light change, lifting away a backdrop, or having certain stage properties, such as a tree or a door,
remain on the stage throughout the performance but used in varying
contexts and functions. By these simple means scene shifting is
indicated while a sense of familiarity is suggested amidst seemingly
random change, as in dreams when an object or a person looks
familiar but not quite identifiable. Strindberg's stage directions for
scene one propose a simultaneous décor that combines a changing
backdrop with standing side wings on which a montage of images
suggests the various milieus of the play. These stage directions
implicitly seek to avoid realism by presenting an abstract montage

to replace the conventional painted scenery, the need for set construction, and disruptive scene changes. As Strindberg explains in an undated note attached to his sketch of the scenery – presumably from 1909 when the Intimate Theatre planned to put on the play – the performance should begin and end with the image of the castle's façade painted on a backcloth and illuminated from behind, while the sides are left in darkness. During the rest of the performance he wanted the façade of the building to recede into shadow and the appropriate details of the side-wings-montage to be highlighted (Strindberg 1988b: 154–55).

Early productions: World premiere in Stockholm, 1907; German premiere in Berlin, 1916

The world premiere of *A Dream Play* took place on 17 April 1907 at the Swedish Theatre in Stockholm, directed by Victor Castegren and with a set designed by Carl Grabow, whose painted backdrops had been used for *To Damascus* I at the Royal Dramatic Theatre in 1900 (see Chapter 5). The production included the Prologue, added to the original script in 1906 for an intended but unrealised performance by August Falck's travelling troupe (Strindberg 1988b: 156–57). Strindberg was fully involved in the preparations for the production, but many of his suggestions – such as the use of back projections instead of scene painting and set construction – were rejected and his stage directions were ignored. His request to use overhead limelight for greater visibility was also denied as a lighting method suitable only for variety shows (Strindberg 1966a: 294). In his *Open Letters to the Intimate Theatre* Strindberg complains about the set of adverse circumstances that resulted in an unsatisfactory performance:

> When Director Castegren had succeeded in getting the play accepted at the Swedish Theater, we began to discuss means of transforming the dream into visual representations without materializing it too much. ... In the text I stated about *A Dream Play* that it should be played with standing sides of 'stylized wall paintings' ... I assumed: changing of the backdrop

> as needed. Castegren went to Dresden. ... There he bought the
> [sciopticon] apparatus, but in the tests here at home (which
> I never got to see, however) it did not measure up to what had
> been promised. When Director Ranft did not want to use the
> *Damascus* system of arch and backdrops, the only thing left to
> do was to 'go to Grabow'.
>
> (Strindberg 1966a: 293–94)

Grabow's designs combined pictorial realism with an all-too-obvious
symbolism. The forestage was 'transformed into a field of red
poppies, the symbol of sleep, while the stage behind it was framed
by an arch, decorated with garlands of poppies, inside which the
dream images appeared and disappeared' (Bark 1981: 84). Reviewers
described a few individual scenes and images from the performance.
Vera von Kraemer, for example, expresses her admiration for 'the
castle that grew amidst a rich flood of flowers and colours' (Bark
1981: 86). C. G. Laurin describes Ugly Edith playing the piano in a
snowy landscape in the Fairhaven scene as an image that 'seems
familiar from our dreams', and he finds the scene at the Riviera
brilliant – 'although the set should have been much better and more
paradisiacal' – in conveying the contrast between the life of the
idle upper class and the brutalised coal workers (Laurin 1914:
300). For each scene, then, a specific painted backdrop and
scenery was installed. In spite of some of the positive comments,
Strindberg felt that 'the construction on stage disturbed the
actors' dedication of spirit and called for endless intermissions;
besides, the whole performance became a "materialization phe-
nomenon" instead of the intended dematerialization' (Strindberg
1966a: 293–94).

The role of Indra's Daughter was created by Harriet Bosse, for
whom it was originally written. She was praised for finding the
right spirit that fit her role as a goddess and also for her fine diction
and her light, gliding gait (Bark 1981: 86). The performance, however, lacked a unified style as the actors alternated between lofty
declamation and natural speech. And even though the same theatre
had produced Maeterlinck's *Pélleas and Mélisande* with Bosse
playing the female lead in 1906 (Bark 1981: 83), critics generally

resisted unconventional and non-realistic efforts. 'I heard it said that the settings ought to be more stylised in order to give an impression of unreality, of dreams', one reviewer contended, 'but then, in such surroundings the actors … would also have to be stylised. And a stylised actor – brrr!'[1]

Following what Strindberg considered a failed first staging of his piece, he and Falck made plans to stage *A Dream Play* at the Intimate Theatre in 1909. Strindberg bombarded Falck with ideas of simplified staging that would both fit the spatial limitations of the theatre and convey the dream-like qualities of the play. Instead of sets, 'which in *this case* cannot reproduce unfixed and moving mirages or illusions', they planned to use a red plush drapery stage where nuances of colours and moods were to be affected simply by lighting (Strindberg 1966a: 294). The performance, however, remained unrealised, and the play wasn't staged again during Strindberg's lifetime. The next performance took place in Berlin in 1916 under Rudolf Bernauer's direction at the Theater im der Königgrätzerstrasse. This production became famous for its fairy-tale rendering of the dream sequences featuring Danish-German scenographer Svend Gade's decorative designs. The realistically painted backdrops were embellished with fantastical sweeping, winding lines and the action was shown through a giant oval-shaped proscenium covered with a dark-blue gauze curtain. Gade's design thus distanced the events from the spectators as pure fantasy and also made them the dreamers of the evolving scenes. In the prologue the gold-clad goddess (Irene Triesch) descended to earth in an almond-shaped, golden glory-machine and at the end returned to heaven by the same means, surrounded by tongues of fire (Bark 1981: 98–103 and Marker and Marker 2002: 61–62).

Gade's scenography for *A Dream Play* was admired even in Sweden, where the Lorenberg Theatre in Gothenburg invited him to install the exact replica of his designs in a production directed by Mauritz Stiller later the same year (Bark 1981: 103 and Kvam 1974: 106). Bernauer's production was considered congenial to the spirit of Strindberg's play also in Germany, where as late as 1921 it was positively compared to Max Reinhardt's dark, expressionistic version (Bark 1981: 98–99). By this time famed for his remarkable productions of Strindberg's *Dance of Death* (1900), *The Pelican* (1907), and *The Ghost Sonata* (1907), in the 1910s Reinhardt was invited to Stockholm to direct *A Dream Play* at the Royal Dramatic Theatre in Swedish. The great expectations, however, soon turned into general disappointment expressed by the Swedish press, as it became apparent that Reinhardt's approach radically differed from Bernauer's. The latter's playful interpretation, combining spectacle and humour, emphasised the theme of redemption, while Reinhardt's dark, nightmarish *Dream Play*, staged in the aftermath of the First World War, presented an allegory of suffering humanity in an infernal shadow world.

Max Reinhardt directs *A Dream Play*: Stockholm and Berlin, 1921

One of the central elements in Reinhardt's (1873–1943) staging in 1921 was his expressionistic use of light to create a spooky, hostile, and stifling stage universe. Combined with the intricate lighting patterns, Reinhardt introduced a choral strategy that underpinned the theme of inescapable suffering. The actors were isolated from one another and from their surroundings by spotlights as they emerged from darkness, and the action of the main characters was watched by groups of spectral figures. At climactic moments only the anguished or menacing faces of these apparitions were illuminated. In the second half of the performance Reinhardt created haunting effects as he brought together individual groups of extras into a threatening crowd whose rhythmic movements were accompanied by angst-filled cries orchestrated to many voices, like a grand oratorio (Kvam 1974: 108–11).

Analysing Reinhardt's notes recorded in his prompt-book – which contains both the Swedish script and the German translation – Kela Kvam traces the director's efforts to preserve the pliable structure of the play and convey a dream atmosphere through a visually metamorphic world. Quick scene changes seem to have been accomplished with the help of black-clad stagehands that removed or set up simple set pieces in the darkened areas of the stage while the action went on in the illuminated areas. Special padding on the actors' shoes would assist noiseless movement. During transitions between scenes, shadowy figures would enter in semi-darkness, but would become agitated only when light hit them. Switching characters' positions during blackouts was another means to create a dream-like milieu (Kvam 1974: 110–11).

Viennese designer Alfred Roller's set consisted of pieces of furniture combined with a succession of realistically painted backdrops in dark colours (Kvam 1974: 121–22). The work photographs of Dramaten show the mechanics of visual transformations indicated by some unchanging compositional elements – such as the door with a clover-leaf hole – amidst the changing stage images (Marker and Marker 2002: 71–73). While the production received mixed reviews, Roller's designs were plainly rejected by critics as un-Swedish. Spectators were clearly appalled to behold what many felt were dark horror scenarios, where they expected to see familiar landscapes – a beautiful Swedish bathing resort as 'Fairhaven', for example. Instead of Roller's 'foreign, dry and colourless constructions', they would have preferred to see the work of such young Swedish artists as Isaac Grünewald or Hilding Linnqvist (Ollén 1961: 408).

The music of Pantscho Wladigeroff, the young Bulgarian composer from Reinhardt's Deutsches Theater in Berlin, was criticised for its lack of dream-like qualities. Critics resented that Reinhardt should have rejected the music of Swedish composer Wilhelm Stenhammar, whose score for A Dream Play had been used in the Gothenburg performance in 1916 (Hedvall 1923: 150 and Kvam 1974: 120). Thus, while Reinhardt's directorial skill in creating a compelling production was acknowledged by Swedish reviewers, a number of elements were heavily criticised. They unanimously complained about the 'foreignness' of the production and rejected Reinhardt's pessimistic vision, which was characterised as 'a transposition into German of the whole atmosphere of A Dream Play' (Marker and Marker 2002: 75). Reinhardt's solution for the ending of the play was vehemently condemned by Swedish critics. There was no redemption by having Indra's Daughter (Jessie Wessel) return to heaven and no Chrysanthemum bursting into a flower atop the burning castle. Rather than offering the hope of liberation from earthly misery, Reinhardt's ending seemed to suggest that the heroine descended into hell. During her final speech she stepped into a pile of burning logs and disappeared through a trap-door in the stage floor while, according to a sarcastic account, 'the castle shone in a Bengal light like the closing ballet in a music-hall show' (Marker and Marker 2002: 79).

The negative reception of Reinhardt's Stockholm production demonstrates how the meanings of plays are shaped by the specific historical moment and the political and cultural climate surrounding the performance. Swedish critics had apparently expected to see their own national *A Dream Play*, and were disappointed when the director invited from Germany, a country still suffering from the effects of a lost war in which Sweden remained neutral, presented his daunting interpretation.

Post-war Berlin audiences were more sympathetic to Reinhardt's dark, anguished view of the play that he described as 'the senseless chaos of a struggling, murderous, and dying world' (Kvam 1974: 120). After his return from Stockholm in late 1921 he staged *A Dream Play* again in Berlin, using Emil Schering's German translation. Here he worked with his own permanent company of actors whose strengths he was familiar with. The Deutsches Theater was renowned for its superb ensemble acting, developed during Reinhardt's leadership. Against the suggestive background images of Franz Dworsky, choreographed mass scenes evolved to the accompaniment of Wladigeroff's music. Rather than a goddess and an outsider visiting earth, Helene Thimig portrayed Agnes as a martyr, a frail and suffering human being. Dressed in black, she stepped out of the darkness into a blaze of light in the opening scene. Eugen Klopfer's remarkable performance was noted for his presentation of the Lawyer as a Christ-figure from the slums, 'a mixture of a man from the lower depths and a ghost' (Marker and Marker 2002: 81). Reinhardt also used casting in ways that strengthened the dream atmosphere. Werner Krauss, the famous character actor, for example, reappeared in five different roles – as the Quarantine Master, the Policeman, the Dean, the Schoolteacher, and one of the coal-heavers (Ollén 1961: 416) – suggesting a metamorphic reality with uncertain identities and ghostly doppelgangers.

Artaud's *A Dream Play*, Paris, 1928

A Dream Play – Le songe, ou Jeu des Rêves – was first staged in
France by Antonin Artaud (1896–1948) as the third of the four
productions of his Alfred Jarry Theatre in Paris in June 1928. At this
time Artaud had a conflict-ridden relationship with the surrealist
poets who, under the leadership of André Breton, sought to express
the unconscious as it revealed itself in dreams, in the chance juxtaposition of disparate images or objects, or in 'automatic writing'
based on free association (see Breton 1978: 1–6). Though the surrealists had expelled Artaud from their circles in 1926 (Swerling
1971:184), his work at this time, including the Strindberg production, shows distinct surrealistic characteristics. While Artaud is
better known for his influential later theories of the Theatre of
Cruelty (see Innes 1993: 59–94), his radical anti-establishment work
as a director at the Jarry Theatre was a milestone in the advancement
of a non-representational mode of performance.

The premiere on 2 June 1928 attracted an illustrious audience,
including the French poet Paul Valéry, novelist François Mauriac,
playwright Arthur Adamov, Swedish artist Isaac Grünewald (who
was later to design sets for Olof Molander's production of *A Dream
Play*), representatives of the Swedish Embassy and members of the
French nobility and cultural elite. A group of surrealists, including
Breton and the poet Louis Aragon, had come in order to disrupt the
performance because Artaud had accepted a subsidy from the
Swedish Embassy. Embracing an anarchist ideology, the surrealists
condemned any association with government agencies and rejected
the theatre in general because it required financial support and
'subordinated thought to money' (Schumacher 2001: 30). As the
performance began, mocking remarks were heard from the auditorium (Swerling 1971: 184). According to eye-witnesses, a riot broke
out during the scene of Christine insulating the Lawyer's house. The
surrealists were hurling abuses at the play, the playwright, and
the theatre. In an attempt to pacify the surrealists, Artaud stood up
and declared from the stage that 'Strindberg is a rebel, like Jarry, like
Lautréamont, like Breton, like me. We perform this piece as a vomit
against his country, against all countries, against society' (Swerling

1971: 185). Feeling insulted, the Swedes, including members of the Embassy, left the theatre. The supporters of Artaud and the surrealists clashed. Finally, the police restored order, arresting four of the surrealists, after which the performance proceeded apparently without interruption and received warm applause (Swerling 1971: 186).

Even under such unfortunate circumstances, Artaud's production of *A Dream Play* had a significant influence on the modern theatre. It represented Artaud's practical realisation of the theories and goals formulated in his manifesto for the Jarry Theatre. The founders, including Artaud, Roger Vitrac, and Robert Aaron, decided to create a theatre 'not in order to put on plays but so that all that is obscure, hidden, and unrevealed in the mind will be manifested in a kind of material, objective projection. We do not seek, as has been done before, ... to give the illusion of what is not, but on the contrary, to present the eye certain tableaux, certain indestructible, undeniable images that will speak directly to the mind.' In order to achieve these goals, everything on stage, the 'objects, the props, even the scenery ... will have to be understood in an immediate sense; ... they will have to be taken not for what they represent but for what they really are. ... [Even] the movements of the actors, must be regarded solely as the visible signs of an invisible or secret language.' This secret language will be born on stage in the immediacy of each gesture which will 'carry behind it all the fatality of life and the mysterious encounters of dreams' (Artaud 1988: 160–61).

A juxtaposition of the manifesto with the programme notes for the production helps us to understand and visualise Artaud's interpretation of *A Dream Play*. The programme notes proclaim that Strindberg's piece 'has a place in the repertoire of an ideal theatre. ... An infinite compass of feelings are brought together and expressed in it. At the same time, we find in it both the outer and inner aspects of manifold, vibrant thought' (Artaud 1971: 68). Such a play resonates with the objectives of the Jarry Theatre, which 'wants to reintroduce into theatre not a sense of life but certain truths situated deep down in the mind. There is a certain interplay of associations in the mind between a real and dream existence.' But, according to Artaud, the theatre of his day only portrays life through realistic sets and lighting that 'attempt to restore the ordinary truths of life or else cultivate *illusion*' by using 'unreal props, flats and painted canvas drops'. With the help of Strindberg's play the Jarry Theatre has chosen a different path, simply by 'showing real objects from real life, by their arrangement, their associations, the relation between the human voice and lighting', which reveals 'a whole self-sufficient reality. … The false amid the real is the ideal definition of such a production. A meaning, a par-ticularity of a new mental order is given to the ordinary objects and things of life' (Artaud 1971: 68–69).

There is little evidence to clarify how the vision of the pro-gramme notes was transposed into the physical reality of the stage. As a director, Artaud created a scenario for each play he planned to stage, a kind of prompt-book, which consisted of his summary-analysis of the script, and a scene-by-scene detailing of sets, props, lighting, sound, movement, gesture, and voice. Unfortunately, the scenario for *A Dream Play* is lost, and so are those of the other three productions that were put on by the Jarry Theatre. Therefore, for insights on Artaud's directorial methods and his characteristic approach to Strindberg one must turn to the extant scenario for a planned but unrealised performance of *The Ghost Sonata* from 1928. Here Artaud is still preoccupied with a 'secret language' that conveys an invisible reality through the physicality of gestures and objects. He notes that Strindberg's characters 'always seem on the point of disappearing, to be replaced by their own symbols' (Artaud 1971: 100). Therefore his production of *The Ghost Sonata* was to be governed by an attempt to physicalise a 'slipping away from reality, this constant denaturation in appearances' by means of

> voices changing tone arbitrarily, overlapping one another, sudden stiffening of attitudes and gestures, lighting changed, decomposed, unusual importance suddenly given to a small detail, characters … being replaced by inert doubles, in the form of dummies, for example, which suddenly take their place.
> (Artaud 1971: 97)

One example of exaggerating small details is when 'certain objects mentioned by Strindberg … take on disproportionate importance.

They grow much larger than life' (Artaud 1971: 101). Sound effects are to be carefully orchestrated so as 'to emphasize their fantastic aspect when necessary, leaving everything on a banal, pedestrian level where it belongs, thus bringing the rest out by contrast' (Artaud 1971: 101). Such sound effects seem to aim at merging several different layers of reality on stage.

The Ghost Sonata scenario also reveals how Artaud developed a *mise en scène* where the play script had no supremacy over other – visual and aural – production elements. Rather, the dialogue became part of a dissonant sound track, as actors' live voices mingled with distorted voices of dummies amplified through loudspeakers, and various other shocking or mysterious sound effects. Exploring Strindberg's influence on the French theatre, Anthony Swerling observes that *The Ghost Sonata* scenario intensifies 'what is already intense' and cultivates 'what is incongruous' as 'his genius merges with Strindberg's to the point of self-identification. ... [Artaud] fertilises Strindberg's play with shapes, colours, vibrations, gestures and pantomime foreign to the playwright, concentrating on sound and rhythm rather than language' (Swerling 1971: 68–69). However improper this treatment might seem, Artaud's production seems to have transposed the surrealist aesthetics onto the stage while embodying the fundamentally Strindbergian revolt against conventional bourgeois theatre. At the same time, his approach anticipated elements of the post-modern theatre of images exemplified by Robert Wilson's production of *A Dream Play* some three-quarters of a century later.

The two extant photographs taken at the performance of *A Dream Play* (reproduced in Swerling 1971) show how Artaud would use spotlights to illuminate certain isolated areas of the stage and create startling effects by 'violent' contrasts. Both photographs reveal a simple set on an almost bare stage: just a curtain in the back and a few individual set pieces. One of the images shows two tall ladders centre stage, stretching into the flies, framed by two symmetrical square spots on the back curtain lit with bright light. Two performers, each sitting on the steps of their respective ladder at different heights, complete a striking, dream-like tableau, a minimalist composition with real objects and people, yet exuding a sense of the unreal. The photo was probably taken during the scene at the Lawyer's office, for Raymond Rouleau, who played the Lawyer, later described how he would bring a ladder on stage and climb to the top of it 'in order to take down his overcoat from a hanger attached to the ceiling' (Marker and Marker 2002: 67). Tania Balachova, who played Indra's Daughter, commented that the 'décor was starkly simplified … it was very real without being naturalistic. Objects were placed in very strange places; it was pop-art in embryo. But this "pop-art" did not give the impression of a music-hall act; Artaud made it poetic' (quoted by Marker and Marker 2002: 68). The other photograph was taken during the Foul Strand episode, and it shows some audience members standing up and turning towards the back of the auditorium, apparently reacting to the disturbances. On the stage Indra's Daughter, the Quarantine Master, and the Officer are seen in front of a starkly lit back curtain, and two white-clad performers are stretched out on symmetrically positioned structures, apparently the 'instruments of torture' on which the overindulged wealthy people exercise. Both photos show the use of sparse set pieces and the back curtain as the main component of the scenery, which, combined with the lighting effects, looks like the so-called drapery stage Strindberg and Falck had experimented with at the Intimate Theatre (see Chapter 6).

In spite of the rioting, the production received overwhelmingly positive reviews. Benjamin Crémieux considered it '[o]ne of the most remarkable and innovative scenic realizations offered by the theatre [in Paris] this year'.[2] This reviewer gives a sense of the production and of Artaud's work as a director in some detail:

> The success of Monsieur Artaud was to create on the stage the surreal atmosphere that Strindberg's work demands and to achieve this through the poetic use of the most quotidian reality. One knows the paintings of De Chirico, those *juxtapositions* of ancient temples, laboratory instruments, and daily objects from which there emanates such huge suggestive power. Monsieur Artaud has adopted a somewhat analogous method, which he has employed to great effect. The décor is composed of some *violently real objects*, whose relationship to each other

or whose relationship to the actors' costumes and to the words they say creates a poetry within them that reaches toward the invisible. The universe Monsieur Artaud succeeds in conjuring up is one where everything assumes a meaning, a secret, a soul. It is difficult to describe and even more so to analyze the effects achieved, but they are really striking. A true reintegration of magic, or poetry in the world.[3]

Although there were only two performances, and even those were fraught with scandal, Artaud's production of *A Dream Play* seems to have made a strong impression and a lasting effect on spectators. Even forty years later, playwright Arthur Adamov affirmed the production's influence on his work, stating in a letter that it was 'Artaud who, with Strindberg ... taught me the primordial role of the stage space' (quoted in Sellin 1968: 92). In the opinion of a Swedish audience member the 'mise-en-scène had been very beautiful, much superior to that of Reinhardt'.[4] According to an official report of the incident by a member of the Swedish Embassy, 'the public was intelligent enough to understand the intrinsic beauty of the play' and 'a sober view of the affair would be that the accompanying violence showed the life-force of this masterpiece and was an excellent propaganda for "our countryman here in France"' (Swerling 1971: 185–86).

Olof Molander's *A Dream Play* productions: Stockholm, 1935; Gothenburg, 1947

Following Reinhardt's Stockholm performance, *A Dream Play* was not staged in Sweden again until Olof Molander's (1892–1966) epoch-making production at Dramaten in 1935. Molander's approach was inspired by Martin Lamm's influential first book on Strindberg (Lamm 1924, 1926) that explored the autobiographical background of each play (see Chapter 1). In a pre-production interview published in the daily newspaper *Dagens Nyheter*, Molander explained his directorial concept. He felt this was the most autobiographical among Strindberg's plays, and claimed that he discovered 'a line – Strindberg's own lifeline' encoded in the text

(Bark 1981: 118–19). Strindberg represented life exactly as he experienced it and therefore 'his dream images have an incredible reality', which justified Molander's realistic – or rather, as he called it in the interview, 'hyper-realistic' – presentation of the play (Bark 1981: 119). While Molander's emphasis on realism was a reaction to what he thought was Reinhardt's exaggerated and subjectively distorted foregrounding of the horrific aspects of life (Bark 1981: 119 and Marker and Marker 2002: 82–83), he also rejected Strindberg's stress on stylisation. Bo Bergman, a respected critic of the period, welcomed this approach because, he wrote, 'dreams do not stylise. They are realistic in their details' (Bark 1981: 119). Strindberg's script was presented in its entirety, only the scene at the Riviera with the coal-heavers was cut in order to preserve the autobiographical continuity.

One of the innovations of Molander's production – directly related to his biographical reading of the play – was his identification of the three main male characters with Strindberg (Lamm 1971: 396–97). Lars Hanson in the role of the Officer presented the author's youthful and passionate alter ego, praised by critics for creating one of the most memorable and – as opposed to Reinhardt's actors fourteen years earlier – the most 'Swedish' characters in the performance:

> His ... face radiated childish goodness and unsuspecting openness, which, with all his silly absentmindedness, made him quite irresistible. His chivalric, blond, Swedish-lieutenant appearance revealed a boyishness, which made it entirely natural for us to discover him again at the school-bench.
>
> (Beijer 1954: 209)

Gabriel Alw, as the Lawyer with a tormented Christ-like face, played the mature Strindberg persona, and Ivar Kåge, as the wise elderly Poet, even wore a Strindberg mask. Contrary to Reinhardt's production, where the Poet was simply one of the anguished and struggling people, Molander gave the Poet the superior role of 'the omniscient consciousness, the artist dreamer' (Marker and Marker 2002: 84). Tora Teje's statuesque Daughter, dressed in black,

contributed to the dream atmosphere when she took the position of
an outsider or spectator, watching from the forestage the dream
scenes enacted on the main stage (Beijer 1954: 208–09 and Bark
1981: 122, 133).

Molander devised three distinct playing areas: a shallow forestage, a deeper middle stage, and an elevated structure in the back,
mainly used for the promotion ceremony and the final procession
(Bark 1981: 120). The set reproduced the milieu of turn-of-the-
nineteenth-century Stockholm and the Stockholm Archipelago
where Strindberg spent much of his youth and to which he returned
in the early 1900s. Sven Erik Skawonius's sets – which consisted of
pieces of furniture and free-standing structural elements such as a
house wall with a window, a gate, or a balustrade – were combined
with Isaac Grünewald's atmospheric backdrop designs, painted on
glass plates and projected onto the cyclorama. Some scenes were
dominated by the projected image, while others displayed only a
corner of a room, illuminated by a spotlight, and the rest of the
stage remained dark. Because of the director's view that dream
images lack colour, Skawonius used mostly shades of black and
white for the set, while the back projections added colour and spe-
cificity to the stage image. Dream atmosphere was created as single
set pieces – a cupboard with a cloverleaf hole in its door for
example – remained on stage for several scenes. Two small
revolving stages side by side were also used to help a smooth,
dream-like transition between scenes such as Foul Strand and Fair
Haven.

Elements of local colour and hints at Strindberg's life could be
found in virtually all of the scenes. Through an arched gate of the
theatre corridor one caught a glimpse of the park and the church
next to Dramaten where Strindberg used to wait for his 'Victoria',
Harriet Bosse. The final tableau of the performance included a cross
with the Latin inscription '*Ave crux spes unica*' ('Hail cross, our
only hope') looming against a collage of human faces projected on
the background. The shape of the cross was similar to the one on
Strindberg's grave on which the inscription reads '*O crux ave spes
unica*' ('Hail oh cross, our only hope'). Since by now all dream
characters, including the Daughter, had disappeared, the Poet

wearing Strindberg's features remained alone on stage in the shadow of his own grave. Thus, while Reinhardt's staging of the play had been noted in Sweden for its 'foreignness', Molander capitalised on audiences' familiarity with the dramatist's life and the Swedish milieus. His production was received enthusiastically by Swedish critics and audiences alike (Bark 1981: 126, 130, 135). As Gunnar Ollén contends, in Molander's staging the Strindberg of *A Dream Play* became

> a Swedish Strindberg who dreamed of the Swedish archipelago and of the turn-of-the-century Stockholm milieu. All the fantastical elements of the play had such a powerful effect, not because, as in the German production [of Reinhardt], they were stressed and made profound, but because they appeared a natural part of reality.
>
> (Ollén 1961: 410)

Among Molander's several revivals of *A Dream Play* it was his post-Second World War production in 1947 at the Gothenburg City Theatre that came closest to Reinhardt's dark, angst-filled vision. At the conclusion of this performance a cross was seen against a 'fiery red horizon, rising above the blackened ruins of a bombed-out city' (Marker and Marker 2002: 91). In the foreground, however, there stood the Poet again (Sven Miliander), still wearing his Strindberg mask. While details of Molander's staging changed over time, the 1935 production epitomises his basic directorial approach to Strindberg's work, which remained tied up with a biographical view of the play.

Ingmar Bergman's *A Dream Play* in Stockholm, 1970, 1986; Mingei Theatre Company in Tokyo, 1978

Ingmar Bergman's first stage production of *A Dream Play* in 1970 at Dramaten in Stockholm offered a radically new understanding of the work. Bergman not only rejected his own approach in the 1963 television production, which he felt was influenced by his predecessors, but also challenged the entire realistic and biographical Molander tradition (Bark 1981: 153). Rather than featuring elaborate sets and scene changes to create dream atmosphere and local colour, Bergman's production was distinctly actor centred. An ensemble of twenty-four actors in forty-three roles presented *The Dream Play*, as Bergman called his version, inviting spectators to witness the making of theatre (Bark 1981: 154). Lennart Mörk's set contributed to this interpretation in a Brechtian manner: rejecting illusion and making spectators aware of the theatrical apparatus behind the stage-world. The performance, in an uninterrupted flow of fifteen scenes, was given at Dramaten's 350-seat Small Stage (Lilla scenen), without a proscenium arch and curtain. The back of the stage was opened up the entire length of the building, so that audiences could glimpse the bare firewalls at the rear, and the overhead reflectors were similarly exposed. The set consisted of a table with a lamp downstage and a row of chairs placed along the rear edge of the stage, where the performers not part of the ongoing scene took a seat and observed the action. Additional set pieces included a few screens that were re-arranged by the actors during transitions between the scenes. Upstage centre, a raised platform stood against the backdrop of an abstract design with winding red lines. Revealing an interesting aspect of theatrical reception, this unspecified decoration compelled reviewers to assign it specific meanings, identifying it alternately with the burning castle, human blood vessels, the fiery interior of the earth or the inside of the eyelid during dream (Marker and Marker 2002: 100). Otherwise, the set was dominated by black and grey with the exception of the Fair Haven scene, when a white curtain was temporarily drawn in front of the elevated platform to create a stage-within-the-stage populated by white-clad actors.

Bergman also made the Poet (Georg Årlin) the central character of his production, but in a quite different sense than Molander. Bergman's staging explored the creative process of the artist: the theatre as it is being born in the Poet's imagination. Dreaming became a metaphor for making art, similar to how Strindberg described the birth of his first play while watching figures emerging in his mind as if on a stage (see Chapter 1). In the opening scene characters from the play entered and started randomly walking about the stage. As the Poet in his dressing gown sat down at the table, the entire cast circled around him in a sombre procession. While he was reading the first lines of the performance, borrowed from Indra's Daughter in the second Fingal's Cave scene, the characters took their seats in the back, waiting for their call:

> The earth is not clean.
> Life is not good.
> Men are not evil,
> Nor are they good.
> They live as they can,
> A day at a time.
>   (Strindberg 1971a: 5)

The Poet then turned to Agnes – the earthly incarnation of Indra's Daughter – whispering, 'Agnes, the castle is still rising from the earth' (Strindberg 1971a: 5), as if a prompter were feeding an actor's lines. Looking around, Agnes repeated the line, which, after some additional prompting from the Poet, made the Glazier (Oscar Ljung) respond. In this way the action was set in motion by the Poet, who assumed the role of the dreamer and the creator of the figures on stage, sometimes reading out the dialogue and the stage directions himself, at other times eavesdropping on the characters from under his table (Bark 1981: 155).

Bergman divided the figure of the Daughter into two distinct characters played by different actors: the earthly Agnes (Malin Ek) and the divine Indra's Daughter (Kritstina Adolphson). The latter, however, turned out to be just a stage role. Namely, Strindberg's Prologue, the dialogue between Indra and his Daughter, was presented as a performance-within-the-performance. Following the scene at the Officer's parental home, Agnes and the Officer found themselves in a theatre where the actors playing Indra's Daughter and the Bard (Bergman's substitution for Indra as an idealised parallel to the earthly Poet) mounted the elevated platform amidst applause from the other performers watching. Following their recitation of the Prologue in a dignified, classical manner, the world of the theatre came alive and the scene in the theatre corridor began (Bark 1981: 157). Bergman thus turned Strindberg's Oriental metaphysics into a metatheatrical reality by staging the Prologue, removed from its introductory position, as a play-within-the-play.

In his adaptation Bergman extensively re-arranged the text by transposing lines and dividing the text into fifteen scenes. Michael Meyer's published English translation (Strindberg 1971a) does not reflect the performance accurately, since many of Strindberg's original stage directions, cut by Bergman, are left in the script, and actions inserted by Bergman are not indicated. At the conclusion of Bergman's version, for example, the Poet spoke what in the original script were Agnes's parting lines and then exited, leaving Agnes alone on the stage with an anxious expression on her face (Bark 1981: 159).

The production received mixed reviews; the substantial cuts and the de-romanticised metatheatrical approach made some critics complain that Strindberg's intended dream atmosphere was sacrificed. Others appreciated that the play was freed from the heavy theatrical machinery and all-too-concrete imagery. Most reviewers seemed to agree, however, that Bergman's version not only challenged the biographical Molander tradition but also offered an altogether fresh interpretation and a fascinating experience relevant for an audience of the 1970s (Steene 2005: 623–24).

Bergman's idea of splitting Agnes/Indra's Daughter into several characters influenced directors internationally. In the 1978 production of the Mingei Theatre Company in Tokyo, directed by Mitsuya Miyauchi, three actresses shared the main part. In each scene one Agnes would take the lead while the other two would watch, as if the self were split into several voices representing different viewpoints. Like Bergman, this Japanese director also introduced the character of the Bard in addition to the Poet.[5]

In his 1986 revival of *A Dream Play* at Dramaten, Bergman again made the Poet (Mathias Henrikson) the controlling consciousness of the performance. The playing area was visually framed on the left by the Poet's corner with bookshelf and desk and on the right by a female figure – who later turned into Ugly Edith – sitting at a piano. The set, designed by Marik Vos, was more elaborate than in the 1970 production and featured a series of back projections by Bengt

Figure 10 Yasuhiko Naitou (the Poet), Ninako Yamaguchi (Agnes 1), Yuu Komaki (Agnes 2), Mari Sakamoto (Agnes 3), and Takashi Inagaki (the Bard) in *A Dream Play*, performed by the Mingei Theatre Company, Tokyo, directed by Mitsuya Miyauchi, 1978. Courtesy of the Mingei Theatre Company.

Wanselius, because, as Bergman said in a pre-premiere interview, 'Strindberg took such pleasure in the stage directions that I think it would be a shame to deprive the audience of them.'[6] Bergman also felt that

> The dream-technique of *A Dream Play* was so new when it was written that it somehow came to overshadow other qualities of the piece. ... Strindberg says that he imitated dreaming, but he never says that he tried to reconstruct it. ... I mean that all of these – dream–poetry–reality – make up the totality of what *A Dream Play* is.[7]

In the same interview Bergman confided that with his current (fourth) staging of the play he sought a new approach and put aside all his previous production notes. Instead, he relied on Strindberg's letters from the early 1900s to open up a new pathway into the world of the play. It became clear to Bergman that Strindberg saw life as a theatrical performance, which he constantly observed and turned into dialogues in which he assumed the principal roles and gave other roles to those around him.[8]

The scenography was naturally affected by the altered interpretation. The shifting backdrop projections included images of gardens, bleak back yards, a snowy landscape for Fair Haven, and even an image of the building at 10 Karlaplan where Strindberg lived at the time of working on the play.[9] The Poet was on stage throughout the performance, imagining events and characters and also acting as a stage director. In the second Fingal's Cave episode, for example, he put on a crown of thorns that he had borrowed from a crucifix: a permanent set piece. He then gave pages of a script to Agnes, read out the stage directions, and the two of them rehearsed the scene in front of Böcklin's painting *The Isle of the Dead* as backdrop, while music was playing from an old gramophone. This was both a metatheatrical and a self-referential hint at Bergman's earlier attempts at staging Strindberg's late plays; more specifically *The Ghost Sonata*, where the set shifts from an upper-middle-class interior to the dark landscape of the Böcklin painting. Several reviewers resented Bergman's parodic treatment of this scene – and of some others – contending that the director made no effort to find a satisfactory solution. In general, the reviews were less positive than in 1970, noting echoes from the previous production and signs of the director's tiredness (Steene 2005: 686).

Bergman now eliminated Strindberg's Prologue altogether and retained only the earthly Agnes, split into three incarnations: the child (Ellen Lamm/Linn Oké), the adult woman (Lena Olin), and the ageing mother (Brigitta Valberg). The mother figure became prominent in the final segment of the production when she was given the role of comforting the principal male characters. The little girl who had been seen in the initial scenes returned for the closing tableau: she sat playing on the floor, while the Poet kept on writing at his desk (Steene 2005: 686).

A scenographer's *A Dream Play*: Jarka Burian and Joseph Svoboda, Albany, NY, 1980[10]

In 1980 *A Dream Play* was staged at the University at Albany, State University of New York by American director and acclaimed scholar of Czech theatre Jarka Burian (1927–2005). In addition to his work as the foremost American expert on Czech designer Josef Svoboda (1911–2002), Burian was also a professor at the Theatre Department of SUNY, Albany. With the thought of giving his students the rare opportunity of working with a world-famous artist, he invited Svoboda, one of the most influential European scenographers of the second half of the twentieth century, as guest designer. But in spite of the excitement aroused by Svoboda's fame in the academic theatre circles of the United States, and enthusiastic reviews in the local newspapers, the project remained virtually unknown beyond the Albany region. The short-run university production could not exert the same influence as Svoboda's other work, done at such mainstream professional venues as the Metropolitan Opera or the Teatro La Scala, normally would. Nevertheless, the Burian–Svoboda collaboration is highly significant in showing what the play could become in the hands of an insightful director and one of the most innovative scenographers of the late twentieth century.

Svoboda, who had been head designer at the National Theatre in Prague, was known for the astonishing effects he achieved by the ingenious use of projections, mirror surfaces, and laser beams, constructing scenic environments that did not simply decorate or illustrate the action but created dramatically charged spaces. One of Svoboda's most well-known innovations was the so-called '*Laterna Magika*', developed for the 1958 Brussels World Fair: a mode of performance in which live actors interacted with filmed performers and with images projected onto a system of multiple screens. The theatre company in Prague that Svoboda had established by the same name perfected the technique so that the live and the filmed environments became indistinguishable, as performers effortlessly inhabited both (see Burian 1971). Svoboda's *Laterna Magika* technology can be seen as a modern realisation of Strindberg's dream of magic lantern projections, which he had envisioned for the world premiere of *A Dream Play*.

Figure 11 Scene from *A Dream Play*, University at Albany, State University of New York, directed by Jarka Burian, scenographer Joseph Svoboda, 1980. The Jarka Burian Papers. Courtesy of the M. E. Grenander Department of Special Collections & Archives, University at Albany Libraries.

Key elements in the Albany production, Burian explained, were a series of shifting projections onto a configuration of three suspended wire screens, which were previously crumpled, and then unfolded and hung up to form three planes dividing the stage space. These screens functioned as either solid or transparent surfaces, depending on the lighting in front of or behind them, onto which the images were projected. Their effect was complemented with the additional projecting surface of a cyclorama at the back of the stage. The images were cast from six projectors, each of which was fed manually with slides that consisted of 15 × 15 cm glass plates, all prepared by Svoboda. The projections, suggesting the various locations of the play, hit the screens at different angles and several images could be projected simultaneously, side by side or partially overlapping. This scenic solution created a layered dream environment while at the same time making possible swift and effortless scene changes (Burian 1980).

The projections were complemented by a few free-standing set pieces on an otherwise bare stage – a door, a window, a table, a cross, a tree, among others – serving various functions in the various scenes. During the performance these set pieces were periodically re-positioned in full view of the audience by a group of grey-clad performers who moved around the stage in slow motion. As they kept re-arranging the environment, the stage image slowly shifted, intensifying the sense of dream-like dissolves created by the projections. At the conclusion of the Daughter's journey, the individual set pieces were arranged in a row as if marking the stations on her path, similarly to the free-standing mansions in the performance of medieval passion plays.

Several reviewers described their impressions of the visual effects in some detail and how the combination of elements – projections, lighting effects, and set pieces moved around by the chorus – created a dream atmosphere. They stressed that Svoboda's work was 'not scenery in the conventional sense, for he has created … an environment, both ethereal and earthy'. The images against the crumpled screens brought forth 'gorges, clouds …, a castle rising from the mud, marbled, tissuey walls, all either abstract or angled, as they would appear in a dream'.[11] One critic described the backdrop, 'upon which fuzzy images of buildings and stormy skies [were] projected, [and which] work[ed] beautifully in conjunction with scrims. … [T]he pink, blue and white light [brought] forth myriad dream shapes on warped surfaces. … [The screens were] used skilfully with the backdrop to create amorphous landscapes, ranging from the pastoral to the nightmare.'[12] One account describes the entire arc of the visual-dramatic landscape:

> The play works its mysterious spell in [the] caverns of the mind, opening in a dazzling cloud cluster of stars and galaxies stretching into infinity, closing with the literally breathtaking image of a rose seemingly suspended in space, its warm red glow complemented by the shadowy figures of the cast stretching the width of the stage, holding lit candles which cast a warming glow.[13]

Burian's 'staggering command of the stage when it [came] to clar-
ifying the dense Strindberg script' was acknowledged as one of the
strengths of the production, as well as his ability to integrate scenography, acting, movement, costumes, and sound in a 'Luminous
Synthesis'.[14] Burian left the text in Evert Sprinchorn's translation
untouched, and, with a cast of over thirty actors, focused on coor-
dinating what was perceived 'a stunning ensemble',[15] rather than on
individual star achievements. On the whole, reviewers found the
production 'a visually and dramatically exciting version', which
'must be seen to be dreamed'.[16]

A Dream Play on the contemporary stage

In the past fifteen years a new generation of internationally working
directors have contributed with their stage versions. In Stockholm
guest directors, Canadian Robert Lepage and American Robert
Wilson, mounted remarkable productions where visual aspects
gained predominance over the text. In London Katie Mitchell and
her company at the National Theatre worked from a new adaptation by playwright Caryl Churchill. These versions attempted what
Strindberg called for in the original Stockholm production in 1907:
to dematerialise the stage and convey the fleeting, dream-like sense
of the human experience.

Robert Lepage, Stockholm, 1994

Lepage's staging of *A Dream Play* in 1994 at Dramaten in Stockholm
took place at the so-called Målarsal, which was converted from a
paint-shop into a flexible space where the stage can be reassembled
differently for each production.[17] The performance was structured
by the continual metamorphosis of a single central image: a rotating
cube, suspended above water and surrounded by darkness. This
approximately three-by-three-metres large, three-sided box enclosed
the playing area, creating a universe of constant motion and dis-
orientation, where humans were struggling to gain a foothold
against the odds of gravity. In this destabilised world of dreams the
floor became a wall, then a ceiling, and the actors needed to train

for weeks to be able to keep their precarious balance. They made their entrances and exits by creeping through a window, climbing a wall to squeeze through a tiny opening up high, or plunging into a gap cut in the sloping floor. 'The cube symbolises architecture, what human beings create in the universe', said Lepage in an interview:

> Around the cube there is nature and life. The symbol of civilisation is a circle around a square. That is why we have rectangular openings on the walls of the cube that lead to the rectangular world that humans have created. The cube rotates like the earth. It also goes around in circles like time. The play must also have a circular rhythm.
>
> (Rosenqvist 1994: 34)

This highly complex scenography, created by Lepage and Dramaten's Jan Lundberg, worked in perfect unison with Bengt Wanselius's projections and the superb ensemble of fifteen actors. Scene changes, as well as the cycles of time, were indicated by the rotation of the cube each time about 90 degrees, either during blackouts or in full view of the audience, while the actors clung on to whatever they could. Space was localised by Ulf Englund's lighting and sound effects and by the projected images that transformed a cave into a theatre or the Lawyer's bleak home. As lights faded up in the Prologue, for example, the audience could see Indra's Daughter (Fransesca Quartey) slowly descending through a greenish-black void, which appeared gradually thickening around her. As the cube rotated it looked as if she was sitting on a slowly turning wheel of life. She was then discovered sleeping on the floor of a stable: a tilted room with brick walls and the sound of horses and birds. As she awakened, she peered through a small aperture in the wall, catching sight of the growing castle, the shadow of which – a plant-like silhouette – fell on the wall. When, at the end of this brief scene, the Glazier left, climbing through an opening in the wall, the cube revolved again while a light change made a little boy in an Officer's cap visible in a corner, sitting by a little table and striking it with his toy sabre. Later, for the scene in Fingal's Cave, the cube rolled into a position with one edge pointing down, creating a diamond

Figure 12 Fransesca Quartey and Gerhard Hoberstorfer in *A Dream Play* at the Royal Dramatic Theatre, Stockholm, directed by Robert Lepage, 1994. Photo by Bengt Wanselius, courtesy of The Royal Dramatic Theatre.

shape, towards a pool of water underneath, while dark-bluish rock formations were projected on the cube's interior. The passage of time was also suggested by Karin Erskine's costumes in a selection of styles representing various periods of the twentieth century. The production as a whole included allusions to the unfolding of the century in the opening year of which Strindberg wrote his visionary play.

Swedish critics unanimously expressed their admiration for the performance, dubbing Lepage a wizard and 'the theatre's poetic renewer'; calling his production 'The poet's *Dream Play*' and 'The best production in the country for several years'.[18] A reviewer of a guest performance in Glasgow praised Lepage for making 'delicate, even-handed use of the religious and poetic imagery in *A Dream Play*, playing Christian motifs – fishing nets, crowns of thorns – against Buddhist-like closed doors of perception, so that Strindberg's work becomes a sustained, compassionate contemplation of human existence'.[19]

Robert Wilson, Stockholm, 1998

As part of the celebrations of Stockholm as the cultural capital of the world in 1998, the American theatre and visual artist Robert Wilson was invited to direct *A Dream Play* at Stockholm's City Theatre (Stadtsteatern). His staging eliminated any trace of a narrative, evoking instead a dream atmosphere by the succession of thirteen tableaux executed in slow motion and accompanied by evocative sound effects and Michael Galasso's haunting music. The acting consisted of precisely choreographed stylised movements, gestures, and emotionally detached intonation. The performers, placed in front of Wilson's stunning back projections, became figures in the overall visual composition in each tableau, and their sometimes distorted, sometimes amplified or echoed voices became part of the sound score. The characters seemed isolated and alienated from their surroundings, following their individual trajectories with marionette-like movements and unawares of the world outside their individual space-time bubbles. Each figure seemed to continually describe the shape of a loop closing upon itself. The dialogue was transformed into fragments of lines from the text, intoned with obsessive repetitiveness at varying pitch and intensity. In Wilson's *A Dream Play* plot evolution and narrative continuity were replaced by visual and aural patterns that produced an aesthetic rather than a dramatic universe.

Wilson had developed the scenography for the production at his Watermill studio on Long Island, USA before rehearsals began. This was then sent to the cast in Stockholm, who had already memorised Strindberg's text. 'Hopefully when these two worlds meet, they will produce a different mental space, something that I could never have invented and Strindberg could never have written,' Wilson told *Dagens Nyheter*'s reporter. 'I try not to illustrate the text in my productions. The visual has its own promptbook, its own laws. There is a tension between what we see and what we hear.' In the same interview Wilson, harking back to the surrealists of the 1920s, explained his preference for clashing incompatible concepts and images. 'If I take this tape recorder and put it on top of a computer, you will see two machines together. But if I put the tape recorder on a stone, it becomes something quite different. It is about putting together the right kind of contrasts that help us see and hear.'[20]

The *mise en scène* included a set of abstract geometrical as well as mimetic elements, which were varied in different combinations both as movement patterns and as backdrop visuals. In the opening sequence Agnes (Jessica Liedberg), like a tightrope walker, descended on a sloping ramp that extended diagonally across the stage into what seemed like a construction site. The back projection in the following scene revealed the Growing Castle as an American colonial-style two-storey house. In the theatre corridor scene a stuffed white horse stood guard by a backlit rectangular, narrow door through which Agnes mysteriously entered. This rectangular shape, imprisoning the figure of Agnes, returned in multiple incarnations as the chairs, table, and metaphoric hairpin of the marriage scene. In the promotion ceremony the academic faculty, dressed like jockeys, performed a grotesque ballet in front of a row of cows being milked. Fingal's Cave was represented by a glowing red brick structure evoking a host of associations, from the Tower of Babel to the forge of Hephaestus, the blacksmith of the gods. But no sooner did one attempt to conceptualise the images, sounds, rhythms, and motions, than a new turn of impressions undermined the seeming coherence. The image of the colonial house recurred in the closing scene as the characters, huddled together on the steps, let go of their attributes – a shoe, a rose, a fishing net – which floated away like so many balloons. Agnes then exited, walking up the slanting beam in the opposite direction to that in the opening tableau.

In Wilson's theatre the text has no supremacy over other components. The verbal, the visual, and the auditory elements work together, or sometimes clash with one another to create a sensory landscape designed to tip over spectators' consciousness into a state of altered perception. One review of the production on tour at the Brooklyn Academy of Music in 2000 comments on the experience:

> Emotions and actions are largely unanchored to language; consequently the Swedish text becomes a component of the sound score. It is the dramatic and sensual aspects of the mise-en-scène that inspire significant visceral revelations and associations, making the English surtitles superfluous. Wilson's use of space and measured time, ... the orchestration of sound ... and evocative lighting resonate far beyond the boundaries of the cerebral.
>
> (Vivier 2001: 499)

Wilson's non-discursive staging seems a perfect match for Strindberg's probing into the unconscious and innovative dream-play technique. But whereas Strindberg searched for a meaning amid an overwhelming sense of disorder, Wilson, by breaking with the conventional hierarchies of performance elements and making unexpected connections, seeks to deconstruct the production of meanings in the theatre.

Katie Mitchell, London, 2005

In conjunction with the exhibition of Strindberg's paintings, drawings, and photography at the Tate Modern Gallery in London in 2005, Katie Mitchell directed a new version of *A Dream Play* at the Cottesloe stage of the Royal National Theatre.

Caryl Churchill's adaptation, based on a literal translation by Charlotte Barslund, eliminated the supernatural context and the mythical and religious references, and updated a number of elements so that they gained contemporary political and cultural relevance. The Growing Castle is turned into a Tower that burns down at the end, the stage/larder door becomes a fridge door, and the four academic faculties are turned into a bishop, a psychoanalyst, a scientist, and a barrister who form the committee of the inquiry dealing with the opening of the door. The Officer receives a knighthood rather than a doctorate, the Solicitor mentions his lawsuit about asbestos poisoning, and Agnes is threatened with deportation as an illegal alien. The coal-heavers show up as construction workers and the Blind Man's son is sent overseas on a warship.

In the preface to her adaptation Churchill confesses her surprise at discovering how political Strindberg was, 'that he was a hero to trade unionists. … When asked what mattered to him most, he said, "Disarmament." He added the coal-miner scene … because there was a miners' strike in Stockholm' (Strindberg 2005: vii). While, accordingly, Churchill's text is replete with references to a post-9/11 globalised world, Mitchell chose to change the focus of her staging completely. She was more interested in the subject matter of dreams and 'those private anxieties we all have: they're tiny details, but they're huge in a dream landscape' (Croall 2005: 6). The play's relevance for her lay in its daring formal experimentation 'done in 1901 without any knowledge of Freud's book *The Interpretation of Dreams*, it's unbelievably radical and extraordinary. It was the first attempt … to do a dream on stage, and even now, over a hundred years later, there are things we as theatre makers can learn from it formally' (Croall 2005: 6).

Mitchell thus interpreted the play, in a literal sense, as dreaming during sleep. In the early phase of rehearsals, the company improvised dreams described in the books of Freud and his pupil and later rival, C. G. Jung. This material then took on a life of its own and shaped the course of the performance. But in order to convince the audience that they are watching an actual dream unfold on stage, the company made the decision to show the dream of one person. The only character in the play with a background story that could serve as a basis for dreaming is the Officer, argues Mitchell (Croall 2005: 7). Therefore, Strindberg's Officer was turned into the stockbroker Alfred Greene (Angus Wright), who became the designated dreamer. The audience saw him fall asleep in his office – set in London in 1950 – and wake up at the end of the performance. Agnes (Lucy Whybrow) was reduced to Alfred's secretary, appearing in his dream as an angel coming to his rescue. Churchill's fridge door metamorphosed into a locked cabinet that stored Alfred's unconscious fears and desires.

Like Wilson, Mitchell took the text – in this case Churchill's adaptation – as a springboard to develop her own performance text. But contrary to Wilson, who used the text as cues for a series of visual and aural responses, Mitchell worked with actors' impulses and intuition to create a dream texture through improvisation. Vicky Mortimer's set, a simple 'composite room' inspired by photos of the old customhouse for New York on Ellis Island, was a covert reference to the quarantine station of Foul Strand in the play (Croall 2005: 12). The thirty quick scene changes in altogether forty scenes were accomplished by using light and a movable wall, which transformed the office into a bedroom, a schoolroom, a theatre lobby, or a ballroom.[21]

Throughout the feverishly paced performance the ensemble impressed critics with 'a tour de force of physical expression', where characters mutated 'into angels, children, dancers and mourners', and 'clever reversals of time, in which scenes [were] replayed backwards, [created] the overwhelming sense that any idea of an ordered world is an illusion' (Kritzer 2005: 504). Several reviewers felt, however, that the poetry and the essence of Strindberg's play were lost. Michael Billington, for example, argued that by presenting the action seen 'through Agnes's eyes, Strindberg showed that "human beings are to be pitied" but capable of human redemption'. But by eliminating the metaphysical framework, the production presented simply an individual dream. Billington felt 'much closer to Strindberg's feverish, disordered imagination looking at his paintings at Tate Modern' than he did 'watching Mitchell's capriciously inventive production'.[22] A. H. Kritzer regretted that the company's virtuoso performances did not compensate for 'the disappointingly small scope of the production', which immersed the audience 'in the subconscious preoccupations of one individual, but never [came] close to engaging with Strindberg's dream of a meta-consciousness that could both encompass and transcend human suffering' (Kritzer 2005: 504). The same reviewer criticised the production also for locating 'desire and suffering squarely within the upper-middle-class milieu' and for staging

> a psychological examination of the desires and frustrations of a member of England's elite rather than a survey of human suffering. Strindberg's representatives of the working class, such as the glazier and the always pasting Kristen, are displaced by an ensemble arrayed in evening dresses, tuxedoes, business suits, ballet costumes, and lab coats. An emphasis on social embarrassment, exclusion, and personal loss replaces Strindberg's concerns with social inequality and division.
>
> (Kritzer 2005: 503)

Post-modern dance theatre: Mats Ek, Stockholm, 2007

For the centennial celebrations of *A Dream Play*'s world premiere, Swedish dancer-choreographer Mats Ek staged his version on Dramaten's main stage, mixing dance with spoken and sometimes sung dialogue. Ek, who is well known in Sweden for his work with the famed Cullberg Ballet Company, has in recent years also served as director in several productions at Dramaten. In *A Dream Play*, as in his previous directorial projects, he combined actors and dancers to inhabit set and costume designer Bente Lykke Møller's visual world. Unspoken thoughts and emotions were expressed through stunning dance sequences, including, for example, the courtship between Agnes (Rebecka Hemse) and the Lawyer (Johan Holmberg), and the love scene between He and She (Joaquin Muñoz and Cecilia Olsen). In Ek's universe dance had a special, healing, and reconciling role that provided a balance against what the director saw as Strindbergian pessimism.[23]

This production was, again, more of an adaptation – by dramaturg Irene Kraus – than an interpretation of the play. The

Figure 13 Scene from *A Dream Play*, The Royal Dramatic Theatre, Stock-
      holm, directed by Mats Ek, 2007. Photo by Roger Stenberg,
      courtesy of The Royal Dramatic Theatre.

mythical-metaphysical framework had been removed, along with
the emphasis on suffering as the inescapable predicament of
humanity. In this production the Daughter's compassion directed
toward people at large had specific objects as well as causes. As Ek
explained, 'Our *Dream Play* is more concrete: it's a pity for me, pity
for him, but there is no generalizing.'[24] Ek's reading aimed at
uncovering 'the play's questions about class, gender, and ethnicity'
by confronting spectators with images of the 'child that almost
strangles the mother' or the genuinely black Quarantine Master, a
character that in Strindberg's text appears in blackface.[25] Anti-
colonialist rap songs and references to the upsurge of racial prejudice
in the post-9/11 era were also interpolated into the script.

At the same time there was a through-line of theatricality in the
production; 'all that [Ek] found in the depth of Strindberg's text,
was filtered through the magic box of the theatre'.[26] Møller's set
recreated Dramaten – the very site of the performance. Its exterior,
familiar to Swedish audiences, became the Growing Castle, and its
staff entrance was the door that concealed the secret of life. Indra's
Daughter descended from the flies swinging on the curtain, to the
accompaniment of booming Bollywood music, and she landed in
front of the theatre-within-the-theatre. Thus the Indian cultural

framing, as a reference to the entertainment industry, was retained, but without the mythical content.

Ek regards Strindberg's play as 'a radical text with [a] fluid form', but one that is burdened by a series of ideas on Buddhism, Christian martyrdom, and the contradictions of life as a consequence of woman's fall.[27] Therefore his staging put many of the original dream sequences into a grotesque and self-ironic light. For example, when the Lawyer was denied his doctoral degree, he wore a pair of Swedish sausages instead of a crown of thorns. The Poet (Jonas Malmsjö) lamented the nonsense of life while taking a dip in a giant, steaming hot tub. The mystery of the universe was debated not by academics, but by representatives of various world religions – a bishop, a rabbi, and an imam – joined by a scientist; all gathered at the UN General Assembly. This farce of an ideological strife became a commentary on social attitudes toward the 'other' – represented by women and immigrants – as the adversaries all united to ostracise the Daughter (a foreigner, coming from India), turning her into a scapegoat for their failure.

Ek's version was a dream about reality and a critique of oppressive and colonialist attitudes. Our alienation from the real world around us while passively succumbing to media-mediated experiences was powerfully conveyed in the scene at the Mediterranean, which looked like an artificial environment created in a film studio. People in bathing suits and sunglasses were reclining in beach chairs while a walk-on passed by in slow motion, carrying the sun. Strindberg's coal-heavers had been updated to oil-rig workers, struggling with a barrel among the leisurely sunbathers, with no one taking any notice, while their live action was broadcast on television monitors.

Ek made the child, born of the marriage between Agnes and the Lawyer, a central figure in the performance. Giving birth – a scene without words interpolated – was portrayed through the image of the mother's body ripped apart, her limbs sticking out, as if crucified, from behind the theatre's façade. The faceless child was played by an adult dancer (Nathalie Ruiz) wrapped in naked skin, a beige cloth, from top to toe. The baby was shown as a burdensome duty carried by the mother throughout her life in a claustrophobic embrace. Even as the latter was about to leave the earth – a worn-out woman in a hospital bed – the child crept after her with worm-like movements. Agnes's journey through life thus became a parable about a woman torn between her vocation in the world and her family. The production tapped into unconscious anxieties that pervade our lives, and focused on how Agnes gradually grew as a person through experiences of love, guilt, responsibility, separation, and social injustice.

Mats Ek's version of *A Dream Play* prompted widely varied responses. Some critics had misgivings about the liberties taken with Strindberg's script and objected that the play was hard to recognise; 'in Ek's hands no text is sacred'.[28] The same review noted that the dance sequences turned some of Strindberg's darker scenes into pure entertainment, and the energetic, often down-to-earth performance style – for instance in the marriage scene between Agnes and the Lawyer – resulted in the loss of the play's dream quality. Many thought, however, that Ek and his company created a brilliant spectacle which eliminated all the allusions to Strindberg's personal life and showed the audience 'their own life backstage', where the Royal Theatre served as a mental space that afforded spectators to easily glide back and forth between dream and reality, 'between the recognisable present and the suspension of time'.[29]

Notes

1 Daniel Fallström, *Nya Dagligt Allehanda*, 18 April 1907, quoted in Bark 1981: 84.
2 *La Gazette du Franc*, 11 August 1928, quoted in Jannarone 2005: 257.
3 Ibid.
4 Quoted in Jannarone 2005: 261.
5 Interview with actress Yuu Komaki (one of the Daughters), Stockholm, 1 August 2007.
6 Elisabeth Sörenson, 'Ingmar Bergman om sitt fjärde Drömspel', *Dagens Nyheter*, 1 April 1986.
7 Ibid.
8 Ibid.
9 Mats Hörmark, 'Spektakulärt Drömspel blir Bergmans fullträff', *Nerikes Allehanda*, 26 April 1986 and Bengt Jahnsson, 'Bergman sätter kniven i Strindberg', *Dagens Nyheter*, 26 April 1986. In fact Bergman

himself famously lived for a time at the same address where *A Dream Play* and *The Ghost Sonata* were written (Steene 2005: 751).

10 For a more detailed discussion of this production see my article 'Svoboda Meets Strindberg in Albany: Jarka Burian's Dream Play Production' in *North West Passage* (v.6) 2009, pp. 121–42. Many thanks to the editors of *North West Passage* for their kind permission to include some of the passages from the article.

11 Ron Jacobs, 'Strindberg's "A Dream Play": A Sumptuous, Imaginative Success at SUNY A', *KITE*, 20 March 1980.

12 Larry Kinsman, 'The Impossible Dream', *Albany Student Press*, 18 March 1980.

13 Doug de Lisle, 'SUNY A Offers Thinking Journey of Ideas', *Troy Record*. Undated cutting, Jarka M. Burian Papers, University at Albany Libraries.

14 Jacobs, 'Strindberg's "A Dream Play": A Sumptuous, Imaginative Success at SUNY A'.

15 Ibid.

16 Ibid.; Bob Goepfert, '"Scenographer" Svoboda at SUNY A: Stage Design Reflects Action', *Knickerbocker News*, 13 March 1980.

17 See www.dramaten.se/Dramaten/Upplev-Dramaten/Teaterlankar/Malarsalen/ (accessed 27 June 2009).

18 *Sundswall Tidning*, 21 November 1994; *Uppsala Nya Tidning*, 14 November 1994; *Aftonbladet*, 13 November 1994.

19 Richard Loup-Nolan, 'Strindberg's Dreamy Box of Delights', *Independent* (London), 27 May 1995.

20 Betty Skawonius, 'Teatermagisterns lektion i tystnad', *Dagens Nyheter*, 18 October 1998.

21 Charles Spencer, '*A Dream Play*', *Daily Telegraph*, 17 February 2005.

22 Michael Billington, '*A Dream Play*', *Guardian*, 16 February 2005.

23 Anna Ångström, 'Indisk filmmusik kryddar naket drömspel', *Svenska Dagbladet*, 20 March 2007.

24 Lisa Boda, 'Ett drömspel om verkligheten', *TT Spektra*, 20 March 2007.

25 Margareta Sörenson, 'Nydrömt', *Expressen*, 25 March 2007.

26 Lis Hellström Sveningson, 'Ett kollektivt flöde', *Göteborgs-Posten*, 26 March 2007.

27 Ångström, 'Indisk filmmusik kryddar naket drömspel'.

28 Karl G. Fredriksson, 'Drömsplet som vinner på att slippa sin Strindberg', *Nerikes Allehanda*, 27 March 2007.

29 Sveningson, 'Ett kollektivt flöde'.

13   *The Ghost Sonata* and Strindberg's haunting legacy

While *The Ghost Sonata* is considered one of Strindberg's least accessible plays, it has earned a position among his most influential and widely produced works internationally. Its compelling theatricality and novel dramaturgy (see Chapter 3) inspired many outstanding productions, from Max Reinhardt's nightmarish expressionistic vision in 1916 to a mysterious puppet-theatre version directed by American theatre artist Roman Paska with the Swedish Marionetteatern in 1993, and Ingmar Bergman's soul-searching swan-song (his last Strindberg production and third-to-last stage production) in 2000. The following sections explore a selection of productions that testify to the play's ongoing contribution to the shaping of the modern theatre.

World premiere: Intimate Theatre, Stockholm, 1907

Strindberg wrote *The Ghost Sonata*, along with the other Chamber Plays, with an intimate stage in mind, but when it premiered on 21 January 1908 at his own Intimate Theatre in Stockholm, the company was unable to tackle the complexities of the play. The young August Falck, who served both as director and as actor playing the Colonel, lacked the means and the sensibility to develop a convincing theatrical expression of the fundamentally subjective world of the play. The company had no set designer and Falck's idea of a drapery stage (see Chapter 2) that afforded a simple but suggestive and atmospheric staging (with the help of lighting) was not implemented until the production of *Queen Christina* later the same year. These circumstances explain why the reception was mostly negative. Some reviewers were appalled by a presentation that they saw as bordering on the ridiculous, and critic Anna Branting asked herself whether Strindberg was deliberately making fools of the Stockholm playgoers (Strindberg 1991: 413). Others were impressed by the play but found it unsuitable for the stage:

> The drama that undeniably makes a deeply suggestive impression when read seems to be completely impossible to perform ... even by the most artistically accomplished actors. ... [Its staging] demands such extensive resources that the Intimate Theatre's Lilliputian stage can by no means provide.[1]

Bo Bergman, a highly respected critic of the time, felt that inherent in the play was the problem of 'dressing up a dream in flesh and blood', which would have required expression of a vision through movement and diction without losing touch with reality (Ollén 1961: 472). It did not seem to help much that for the premiere Strindberg provided the play with the subtitle 'A fantasy' in order to shepherd audiences away from conventional expectations and suggest instead a kinship with dream-like fairy tales.

Strindberg's composition of a journey – from the external to the internal, from the material to the spiritual – was not followed by the staging. While no descriptive details from Act I have survived, critics complained about the perplexing scenery (Bark 1981: 88). Both Acts II and III were performed with the same set: a bourgeois salon in art nouveau style. Instead of a projection of Böcklin's painting *The Island of the Dead*, as the stage directions would have it, the performance concluded with the opening of a double door at the rear of the stage onto a painted landscape with pine trees. The so-called ghost supper in Act II seemed to critics the most successful in creating a haunted atmosphere, especially thanks to Svea Åhman's 'strongly suggestive' Mummy.[2] In the final movement Anna Flygare, who gave a 'soulful, refined, and artistically interesting' presentation of the Young Lady, 'the ailing human hyacinth',

distinguished herself as the most poetically effective of the performers.[3] Yet the final act seemed just as confusing to critics, who felt
that 'the atmosphere was hopelessly shattered' when the actors were
made to 'discourse about food and servant problems in stylised,
sepulchral tones, [only] to be interrupted all the time from the
kitchen by the Evil One herself'.[4]

Overall, the acting style of the company seemed to reviewers
artificial, affected, and lifeless – an impression that was enhanced by
the performers' monotonous declamation and universally chalk-
white make-up, which made them look 'really starved'.[5] Added to
this was the stiff, marionette-like movement – the actors were
compared to wooden dolls, mannequins, and automatons – carried
out most consistently by Helge Wahlgren as the Student (Bark 1981:
88). But perhaps this was an attempt to imitate the hieratic style of
the Théâtre de l'Oeuvre, the Parisian company that had visited
Stockholm with Maeterlinck's symbolist play *Pelléas and Mélisande*
in 1894. Although Wahlgren could hardly have seen this performance, as he was only eleven at the time, it is telling that his debut
role was Pelléas opposite Manda Björling's Mélisande, when August
Falck's company staged the piece in the city of Malmö before they
moved to Stockholm and formed the Intimate Theatre (Strindberg
1992: 761, 792). In this light, the apparently conscious choice
observed by the entire cast to follow a non-realistic, presentational
acting style, though clearly inconsistent with the realistic drawing-
room set, seems an attempt to create a mysterious, Maeterlinckian
atmosphere. Even so, the critical reception of the production reveals
that neither the Stockholm public of 1908, nor the members of the
Intimate Theatre, were ready to embrace or more fully explore the
unconventional staging opportunities inherent in *The Ghost Sonata*.
Though in 1909 Strindberg proposed to Falck a revival with a
completely non-mimetic drapery stage where the Mummy would sit
in a fold of the curtain (Bergman 1967: 32), this initiative remained
unrealised. While the Intimate Theatre settled in a subdued and
simplified realism for their later work, it was the eclectic and radical experimenter Max Reinhardt who first came to uncover the
astonishing theatrical power of *The Ghost Sonata*, nearly a decade
after its world premiere.

A theatrical revelation: Max Reinhardt's *The Ghost Sonata*, Berlin, 1916

Max Reinhardt's 1916 production of *The Ghost Sonata* – titled in German *Gespenstersonate* – at the Kammerspiele in Berlin, which toured in Stockholm and in Gothenburg in 1917, came as a stunning revelation for the Swedish public. Reviewers found it ironic that the German theatre would teach the Swedes what theatrical potential laid hidden in their countryman's work (Ollén 1961: 472). Reinhardt had already commenced staging a series of the Swedish dramatist's post-Inferno plays, starting with *The Dance of Death* in 1912 (a few months after the playwright's death), *Thunder in the Air* in 1913 and *The Pelican* in 1914. Following *The Ghost Sonata*, he went on to produce *The Burned House* in 1920 and *A Dream Play* in 1921. Reinhardt's Strindberg cycle not only made the playwright a household name in Germany while opening the eyes of his compatriots to the extent of his contributions, but also brought international fame to Strindberg's work, to a much greater extent than ever before. In turn, it was through staging these plays that Reinhardt worked out his own 'expressionist' staging style, which became the hallmark of his productions between the late 1910s and 1920s, and which helped him to establish himself as a quintessentially modernist director (Bark 1981: 103). In these productions Reinhardt gradually developed a stage vocabulary – manifested through sets, costumes, sound effects, lighting, and acting style – that presented a terrifying, macabre world as the physicalisation of an inner reality, that of the playwright, the director, or a stage character. The eschatological vision proffered by *The Ghost Sonata* made the play especially relevant in the Germany of 1916 in the throes of the Great War.

Reinhardt's new approach was apparent already at the onset of the performance: he created a milieu that resembled the real world but was shown from the warped perspective of a nightmare (Kvam 1974: 72). An unearthly atmosphere prevailed throughout the performance. In accordance with Strindberg's stage directions, designer Gustav Knina placed a façade of a modern city dwelling at the back of the stage, with an entrance in the middle and a balcony bulging over it, and with rows of windows on both sides of the entrance door (see Bark 1981:109). But the house was given a surreal dimension by its imposing size and overblown ornamentation, which turned it into an ominous colossus that resembled a living organism (Kvam 1974: 72). Whereas Strindberg's initial stage directions describe a bright Sunday morning, the curtain in Reinhardt's production was raised to reveal a stage enveloped in darkness, which only gradually gave way to faint grey light and revealed dark, motionless figures, suggesting a shadow world. As if awakening from a death-like slumber, the figures slowly came to life, but still without talking, while church bells and organ music could be heard in the distance. Throughout the performance a brighter light was introduced whenever the Student (Paul Hartmann) entered, but in his absence the semi-darkness returned and the shadows took possession of the stage. The Student was further set apart from the macabre shadow world around him by reacting to his terrifying 'visions' with gestures of bewilderment, passing his hand over his eyes as if watching a bizarre dream. Throughout the performance this gesture punctuated his encounters with the supernatural, when, for example, he saw the Dead Man walking the street or the group of beggars at the conclusion of Act I soundlessly miming applause and mouthing cheers. Clearly Reinhardt cast the Student as the dreamer whose perspective was shared with the spectators as he moved around like a sleepwalker and his vision as a clairvoyant 'Sunday child' shed light on the secret shadow life of the dead (Marker and Marker 2002: 124 and Bark 1981: 114).

Act II was set up as an oval salon, with an imposing tiled stove upstage centre and an oval table with chairs at the middle of the stage. The dark-violet furniture was enclosed by mould-green walls and the gloomy semi-darkness brightened only briefly as the Student walked through the salon to the next room. Reviewers were taken by 'the strange nightmare of marionettes' in the ghost supper scene. 'It was as though something behind and beyond the human held the strings of all these puppets with their mechanical and stylised movements', commented Bo Bergman in *Dagens Nyheter* (quoted in Marker and Marker 2002: 125). Gertrud Eysoldt as the Mummy was considered exquisite as she portrayed both the human and the parrot-like aspect of her character with great subtlety. The room of

Act III was decorated with potted hyacinths along the walls and the grey and violet hyacinth patterns with gold ornament were repeated on the wallpaper, echoed by the colours of the Young Lady's dress, 'to indicate [her] withering, half incorporeal nature'.[6] As the vampire Cook appeared in the hyacinth room, the Young Lady (Roma Bahn, in Stockholm Else Eckersberg) started to turn into the Mummy (her mother), adopting the latter's mannerisms, and thus becoming more and more like the rest of the 'ghosts'. By the conclusion of the performance only the Student remained exempted from the spectral world of the dead. Whereas Reinhardt's promptbook suggests that he had considered making the Student in the third act resemble the Old Man, reviews of the actual performances do not confirm that transformation. In Paul Hartmann's performance they note instead the character's youthfulness, his love of truth, and the horror he expressed when encountering inexplicable evil (Bark 1981: 114).

The greatest sensation of the production was Paul Wegener as the malicious Old Man, Hummel. He transformed the character into the embodiment of a sheer demonic force, a dreadful vampire who grew in strength as he fed on others. In his prompt-book Reinhardt describes him appearing initially small, disfigured and lifeless like a corpse. While he talks to the Student over the course of Act I, he begins to expand as if he drew strength and life from the young man, and by the time he enters the round salon in Act II, he has grown horrifyingly large. Reviewers' accounts support the descriptions of the prompt-book: 'With his shrunken, stony face and crumpled posture as he sat there in his wheelchair banging his crutches and croaking in a hoarse voice, he left an impression as chilling as the barren coldness of a dead soul,' commented one critic of the Hummel of Act I,[7] while another described his entrance in the following act:

> As Hummel stood in the doorway, wearing a tall hat and spying with a piercing and distrustful gaze, supported by his dreadful crutches which he clutched in his black-gloved hands, one was certain that all-destroying adversity in person had made an entrance.[8]

Even Reinhardt's production rejected Strindberg's direction of making *The Island of the Dead* the final image. Instead, desperate for a breath of fresh air in a claustrophobic world of decay, the Student threw open a window during the concluding sequence. As the room seemed to submerge in the dusk of death, he recited his final lines while a shaft of otherworldly white light streamed in through the open window, revealing the starry firmament (Bark 1981: 115).

American premiere of *The Ghost Sonata*: Provincetown Playhouse, New York, 1924

In 1916, when Reinhardt staged his *Gespenstersonate* in Berlin, American dramatist Eugene O'Neill had the first productions of his early plays at the small non-profit venture called the Provincetown Players in Provincetown, Massachusetts. Created by a group of young writers, directors, and designers as a revolt against the commercialisation of cultural institutions such as the theatre, the Provincetown Players soon moved to Greenwich Village in New York, further nurturing the work of such American playwrights and poets as O'Neill, Susan Glaspell, Wallace Stevens, and many others (see Ranald 1984: 397–99). But the original group disbanded in 1922 and the company was re-organised in 1923 as the Experimental Theatre, Inc., under the management of the so-called triumvirate including critic and theorist Kenneth Macgowan, designer Robert Edmond Jones, and Eugene O'Neill. Though the company still performed at the so-called Provincetown Playhouse at 139 Macdougal Street in Greenwich Village, its programme changed radically under the new leadership. More emphasis was now placed upon professional production values, effective management, and a distinct theatre aesthetic, which combined interest in new stagecraft with a commitment to collaborative experimentation influenced by such European theatre artists as Gordon Craig and Max Reinhardt (see Ranald 1984: 211–13, 398–99 and Deutsch and Hanau 1972: 94–102). The repertoire was now expanded to include both American and European modern plays as well as the classics.

The inaugural production of the Experimental Theatre, Inc. – which opened on 3 January 1924 – was Strindberg's *The Spook*

Sonata in Edwin Björkman's translation. The company's alignment
with a progressive, experimental path pioneered by Strindberg was
highlighted by O'Neill's programme note, entitled 'Strindberg and
Our Theatre':

> In creating a modern theatre which we hope will liberate for
> significant expression a fresh elation and joy in experimental
> production, it is the most apt symbol of our good intentions
> that we start with a play by August Strindberg; for Strindberg
> was the precursor of all modernity in our present theatre. ...
> Strindberg still remains among the most modern of moderns,
> the greatest interpreter in the theatre of the characteristic spiri-
> tual conflicts which constitute the drama – the blood! – of our
> lives today.
>
> (reprinted in Deutsch and Hanau 1972: 191)

O'Neill goes on to denounce the 'old naturalism' and calls Strindberg's
achievement 'supernaturalism'. *The Spook Sonata* thus provided a
programme for the Experimental Theatre, Inc.:

> We are ashamed of having peeked through so many keyholes,
> squinting always at heavy, uninspired bodies – the fat facts –
> with not a nude spirit among them; we ... [pass on] to some as
> yet unrealized region where our souls, maddened by loneliness
> and the ignoble inarticulateness of flesh, are slowly evolving
> their new language of kinship. Strindberg knew and suffered
> with our struggle years before many of us were born. He
> expressed it by intensifying the method of his time and by
> foreshadowing both in content and form the methods to come.
> All that is enduring in what we loosely call 'Expressionism' –
> all that is artistically valid and sound theatre – can be clearly
> traced back through Wedekind to Strindberg's *The Dream Play*,
> *There Are Crimes and Crimes*, *The Spook Sonata* ...
>
> (Deutsch and Hanau 1972: 192)

O'Neill identifies *The Spook Sonata* as one of Strindberg's most
difficult 'behind-life' plays and sets up the company's mission as a

search for truth in the theatre by tackling such difficult tasks as the staging of this play (Deutsch and Hanau 1972: 192).

The Provincetown Playhouse was a small theatre, converted from a space that was once a stable, with architectural features not unlike the Intimate Theatre in Stockholm. The auditorium had wooden benches seating two hundred and it had a small proscenium stage. In 1920 a plaster dome cyclorama, the first in New York City and modelled on those in use at European art theatres, had been installed to allow the creation of special effects, such as projections or the silhouetted dream sequences in the production of O'Neill's *The Emperor Jones* (Deutsch and Hanau 1972: 61–69). Before its first season with the re-organised company, the theatre was again refurbished, and its stage was enlarged with an apron and proscenium entrances.

The Spook Sonata was co-directed by Robert Edmund Jones and James Light and co-designed by Jones and Cleon Throckmorton. Light also played the character of the Dandy, while Stanley Howlett created the role of the Old Man and Clare Eames that of the Mummy. The production testifies to the company's serious investment in experimentation and new stagecraft. A still photo of the ghost supper scene shows the stage with a curved edge and the narrow apron one step down.[9] The set is framed by a pair of side wings, and the statue of the Mummy as a young woman stands upon a bulky pedestal, which also served as the Mummy's closet, upstage centre. In the back the open cyclorama is visible, suggesting the hazy depths of a shadow world as a backdrop to the spectral figures. Some of the supper guests wear masks built by James Light, as an externalisation of the play's themes of pretence and unmasking. In this respect it is interesting to note that Jones and Kenneth Macgowan, the third member of the producing triumvirate, had published the findings of their European tour in 1922 entitled *Continental Stagecraft*, and Macgowan had co-authored (with Herman Rosse) an anthropological study entitled *Masks and Demons* (1923, see Ranald 1984: 398). While the masks and death screens were all white, the stage was described as enveloped in 'a symphony of ghostly blues', which lent the production a 'sepulchral, funereal dimension' (Wainscott 1997: 127).

Following *The Spook Sonata,* productions of Strindberg's plays on the commercial stages of the United States remained scarce, but the Experimental Theatre, Inc., under the leadership of James Light, proceeded to put on the American premiere of *A Dream Play* in 1925. This performance was, however, artistically much less satisfying because of financial and organisational difficulties within the group (see Deutsch and Hanau 1972: 141–42).

The reception of *The Spook Sonata* varied from the enthusiasm of reviewers favouring the experimental theatre movement, who called it a 'milestone' in the New York theatre season, to critics representing the establishment, who dismissed Strindberg's 'sickly phantasies in their strange garb'.[10] The production, however, not only became the company's strong artistic statement introducing its first season, but also deeply impacted the subsequent work of American avant-garde theatre artists and playwrights, most immediately that of O'Neill. In his plays to follow he used masks as well as long, eerie silences that had characterised the ghost supper scene, enhancing their expressiveness (see Ranald 1984: 398 and Wainscott 1997: 128). And, perhaps most importantly, the performance helped to advance an American experimental theatre seeking alternatives to the mainstream commercial production values glorified by Broadway.

Made in Sweden

Olof Molander's The Ghost Sonata, *Stockholm, 1942*

The Ghost Sonata finally became naturalised in the Swedish mainstream theatre by Olof Molander's landmark production in 1942 – the first of his five revivals of the play – at the main stage of Dramaten in Stockholm. In sharp contrast to Reinhardt's macabre expressionistic version seen in Sweden in 1916, Molander treated the text – as that of *A Dream Play* before – as the dramatist's covert autobiography, and set it in a hyper-realistic turn-of-the-century Stockholm milieu. He aimed at showing how Strindberg's imagination took inspiration from his everyday environment. Sven Erik Skawonius's scenery for Act I featured a photographically accurate

reproduction of Strindberg's apartment house at Karlaplan (demol-
ished in 1969). Apparently, Molander himself lived in the same
street in a similar apartment house, typical of the well-to-do
Östermalm district. Audience members experienced the set as a
slightly over-exposed colour photograph: at once strikingly real and
possessing 'a dreamlike clarity of shading and contour'.[11] Richard
Bark points out the shocking effect of this set upon the theatre-
going Stockholm middle class of the 1940s, for whom the building
represented not an artefact of the past, but their own surroundings,
which seemed to them at once stunningly real and disturbing. The
performance thus transcended the biographical and turned the stage
into a mirror image of the auditorium (Bark 1981: 142). Reviewers
raved about Molander's ability to present a *mise en scène* simultaneously banal and peculiar, real and surreal, as if the building were
animated by the eerie life of waxworks under the shifting light of
the day. A host of mingling street sounds typical of the play's
period – the chiming of church bells, clatter of hoofs, and
approaching thunder – contributed to this double sense of the
mundane and the supernatural (Ollén 1961: 473).

The round salon of Act II was presented as an elegant but foreboding interior where the Colonel's study could be seen as he sat at
his desk on a platform upstage right, while the Mummy's statue and
the opening to the hyacinth room were visible on the left. The room
of the third movement showed a stuffy interior where pots of hyacinths were placed on steps running along the walls, guarded by a
Buddha statue on a pedestal. At the conclusion of the performance
the claustrophobic set opened up as the walls of the room – two
panels touching upstage centre – turned on their pivot and disappeared from sight, leaving the free-standing set pieces on stage
against a black background. The Student, 'Humankind itself', then
walked into the infinite darkness revealed beyond the walls (Bark
1981: 150). This 'hymn-like' conclusion was seen by many as an
expression of yearning for reconciliation and peace: a religious
transcendence of contradictions and a spiritual liberation (Marker
and Marker 2002: 139).

Rather than a diabolical monster, the Old Man was presented in
Molander's production as an ordinary, if unpleasant, person. Lars

Hanson for the first time portrayed the character as vulnerable, uncertain, and even fearful at times. Märta Ekström created a grotesque Mummy in whom a 'spooky coquettishness was mixed with senility' (Ollén 1961: 473). The scene between the Student (Frank Sundström) and the Young Lady (Inga Tidblad) was enacted with tenderness, stressing the poetry of their lines (Bark 1981: 149). Molander's interpretation was widely acclaimed in Sweden, as critics felt that he understood, better than Reinhardt, the true nature of Strindberg's world and did away with the latter's 'conjuring tricks' and 'Strindberg mystique' (Marker and Marker 2002: 139). In the programme note to his 1954 production of the play the young director Ingmar Bergman commented on 'the great, totally shattering experience' of Molander's staging in 1942, which seemed to him 'absolute and totally unattainable' (quoted in Marker and Marker 2002: 132).

Ingmar Bergman's The Ghost Sonata *productions: Malmö, 1954–Stockholm, 2000*

Bergman claimed to have first read *The Ghost Sonata* at age twelve, when he was fascinated by what he later called the play's infantile elements, including such scary characters as a mummy in the closet and a dead man walking (see Törnqvist 2000: 117). As an adult, he staged the play in Stockholm a year before Molander's groundbreaking production, albeit with an amateur company, the Sago Theatre, which mostly catered to children (see Törnqvist 2000: 118 and Steene 2005: 495–96, 498). Whilst his first professional production of the play on the main stage of the Malmö City Theatre in 1954 was admittedly a tribute to Molander (Törnqvist 2000: 118), Bergman's distinct directorial persona was already noticeable. In this production the Student (Folke Sundquist) appeared as the dreamer of a series of strange visions whose dream-like quality was signified by a transparent scrim separating the stage from the auditorium. Though the recognisable Stockholm burgher milieu, introduced by Molander, was retained, the Student was dressed and acted like a youth of the present day, and was even seen by some as Bergman's alter ego. The voluminous and almost jovial Old Man

(Benkt-Åke Benktsson) was also identified with Bergman as he sat at the edge of the stage in Act I introducing the Student into the secrets of the house, like a dispassionate master director (Törnqvist 2000: 119). But the Student–Old Man relationship could have also mirrored that of the young apprentice Bergman and the accomplished director Molander. In either way, the production clearly shows Bergman's early interest in metatheatricality, which he continued to engage with in his mature work in the form of an ongoing commentary on the theatre as a model for the creative processes of the artist.

In his 1973 production of *The Ghost Sonata* on the main stage of Dramaten, Bergman arrived at a distinct interpretation, which is discussed in elaborate detail by Egil Törnqvist, who followed the rehearsals (Törnqvist 2000: 120–40).[12] The entire play was given without an intermission, scene changes were indicated by flickering

Figure 14 Gunnel Lindblom, Elin Klinga, and Jan Malmsjö in *The Ghost Sonata* at The Royal Dramatic Theatre, Stockholm, directed by Ingmar Bergman, 2000. Photo by Bengt Wanselius, courtesy of The Royal Dramatic Theatre.

lights, and a black-and-white photograph of the ageing Strindberg was projected onto the curtain between the acts. But rather than serving as a biographical reference, the projected photograph of the author suggested that we are entering a dream world envisioned by the playwright – with no particular character assigned the role of the dreamer (Marker and Marker 2002: 150–51). Bergman's production radically switched attention from Molander's photographic realism and emphasis on the detailed *mise en scène* to a typically Bergmanesque focus on the actor. No painstakingly reconstructed recognisable locales took away attention from the actors' interactions. Bergman used few props and a simple, stylised set by Marik Vos, consisting mainly of projections, which allowed spectators to focus on the performers.

At the heart of Bergman's interpretation lay the correlation between the Student and the Old Man respective to the Young Lady and the Mummy. In Act III the Student (Mathias Henrikson), whose facial features resembled those of the Old Man (Taivo Pawlo), turned into a brutal aggressor. He literally killed the Young Lady by sexually assaulting her during his unmasking speech. Bergman cast Gertrud Fridh in the double role of the Mummy and the Young Lady. Over the course of Act III the Young Lady gradually transformed into the Mummy, assuming her mannerisms of speech and gesture. At the conclusion the Mummy entered again to pronounce the final speech of benediction (the Student's lines in Strindberg's text) over the corpse of her former self (see Törnqvist 2000: 130). In this way Bergman succeeded in integrating the third act, which he had always felt the most problematic part of the play. As reviewers observed, the closing sequence of the performance suggested 'the law of eternal repetition', showing how the young people inevitably became spiritual heirs of their parents' guilt, deception, and destruction – a basic pattern of bourgeois family life (Marker and Marker 2002: 155).

Bergman's final revival of *The Ghost Sonata* in 2000 at Dramaten's Målarsal, with less than two hundred seats, returned to the intimate format for which the play had been devised. Bergman arrived at an utterly simplified and stylised *mise en scène* with a minimalist set by Göran Wassberg. In his programme note Bergman called the production, after Strindberg, 'A Fantasy', suggesting the imaginary character of what appeared on stage. As the action moved toward innermost spaces of the imaginary building, a projection of a bourgeois house's façade on the black-curtained sidewalls dissolved into an image of hyacinths. Bergman's use of a practically bare stage allowed him to show the foreboding exterior and the gloomy interior simultaneously. The main acting area on the stage was marked out by a green carpet, with a few chairs used as the only set pieces besides a grandfather clock and a statue on a pedestal on the edge of the stage at either side. In this way the audience was positioned in the space of the action as if watching events unfold on the street from inside the house in Act I, and then peering into other rooms in Acts II and III. The viewers' inclusion into the scenic space was suggested already in the opening sequence as the Student (Jonas Malmsjö) entered from the dark auditorium, crawling up on the stage where he then collapsed and was awakened by the apparition of the Milkmaid, so that with him, the audience would watch a waking dream. The stage was surrounded on three sides with a black curtain, which hid the Mummy's closet stage right. In Acts II and III the curtain at the back opened, revealing a small inner stage that allowed a view into another 'room'. During the ghost supper, for example, the young couple was seen sitting there against a green background, the Student clasping a red book to his heart, and the Young Lady (Elin Klinga) tending a flower-pot of hyacinths. This flower-pot, the Young Lady's attribute which she carried with her at all times, was brought to the green playing area in Act III, indicating a change of location into the hyacinth room. The round salon of the previous act was moved to the back, where the Mummy and the Colonel were seen seated in the inner stage against a red background. A sense of witnessing a play-within-the-play was further enhanced when characters positioned outside the playing area intently watched the action on the carpet unfold. In Act III, for example, the Cook (Gerd Hagman) and the servant Bengtsson (Erland Josephson; polishing his master's boots as Jean in *Miss Julie*), representatives of the working class, stood by menacingly, observing the courtship between the Student and the Young Lady, before they interfered and uttered the Cook's lines of threat in unison. The simple set thus made possible a metatheatrical arrangement through an intricate layering of the performance space.

In combination with the stylised, non-mimetic scenery, the make-up, costume (designed by Anna Bergman), choreographed movement (by Virpi Pahkinen), and Béla Bartók's *Music for Strings, Percussion and Celesta* helped to physicalise the world of the play. Props such as the Young Lady's hyacinth pot assumed multiple connotations. Inside the green rectangular playing area she placed the flower-pot in front of herself, as if sitting in a boat, thus evoking the sense of a journey. Such expressively choreographed bits of added physical action alluded to the sonata's leitmotifs and their variations, translating the play's musical structure into visual terms. In Act I the Caretaker's Wife emptied a bucket of human excrement into the sewage drain underneath the stage floor, not far from the hole for the drinking fountain, visualising the theme of being contaminated at the roots of life. The ghost supper guests in Act II exhibited grotesque physical deformities, showing their true nature behind their social masks. The Mummy (Gunnel Lindblom) fluttered about with unkempt hair, wearing a fluffy dress in the colour of dried blood. The Old Man's (Jan Malmsjö) hands were wrapped in dirty, blooded cloth, a reminder of his crimes. The interaction between the Young Lady and the Student in Act III turned into a desperate physical struggle. Submitting to the violence as the Student unmasked her, the Young Lady agonisingly shed her light-blue dress, moving like a wounded bird, to reveal a blood-stained, greyish-white petticoat, and cuts and bruises on her arms. The dried blood on her undergarment around her womb not only connected her with the Mummy, her mother, but also alluded to what the Student called her illness at the very source of life. Following the Student's exit through the audience, the Mummy stepped forward to recite the final blessing over her daughter's body. The Milkmaid then entered rolling down the stage, and remained lying on the floor next to the Young Lady. As the latter's body was carried out, the Milkmaid rose as if the soul awakened from the ashes of the deceased, and performed a soaring dance as the coda to the performance.

Bergman's last production of *The Ghost Sonata* was received with enthusiasm for his unquestioned mastery of the stage (Steene 2005: 752–55), but Swedish critics were struck by a sense of despair, 'the heavy, black and anxiety-ridden world' he depicted, which gives a 'synopsis of a whole Swedish tradition but painted in a dark vision of sulphur and vitriolics', wrote Lars Ring in *Svenska Dagbladet*.[13] Some reviewers saw the production as the ageing Bergman's (eighty-two at the time) 'final farewell. A moment of goodbye so bitter and at the same time so moving that one is close to crying'.[14] Commenting on the guest performance at the Brooklyn Academy of Music, Gautam Dasgupta noted, 'Strindberg's visitation upon Bergman affords yet another glimpse of art as exemplary of spiritual empowerment and moral regeneration' (Dasgupta 2001: 69).

Centennial production of The Ghost Sonata, *Intimate Theatre, Stockholm, 2007*

The centennial of Strindberg's Intimate Theatre in Stockholm was celebrated with a production of *The Ghost Sonata* directed by Richard Turpin, which opened on 6 December 2007 at the same locale where it was seen a century before. Though the first production of the original Intimate Theatre in 1907 was *The Pelican*, current Artistic Director Ture Rangström chose to celebrate with the Chamber Play Strindberg valued highest, which is also one of his theatrically most experimental works. While the original production earned no critical acclaim, this time the performance was appreciated by both reviewers and spectators: it was played to full houses, and, in contrast to such renowned institutions as Dramaten or the City Theatre, to overwhelmingly young audiences.[15]

Turpin, who had directed the inaugural production of Strindberg's *The Freethinker* at the reopening of the Intimate Theatre in 2003, explained in an interview his views on *The Ghost Sonata*:

> At the first reading ... one feels: Wow! At the second: Uh-oh! At the third one asks oneself: How can it be done? At the fourth reading one feels hopeful again. When it comes to *The Ghost Sonata* one must forget everything that has to do

Figure 15 Hans Sandquist and Linda Kulle in *The Ghost Sonata*, at the remodelled Intimate Theatre, Stockholm, directed by Richard Turpin, 2007. Photo by Mats Bäkler, courtesy of Strindbergs Intima Teater.

with stage logic. One needs to find one's own world [in the piece]. … Dramaturgically [the play] is a failure, it makes promises that it does not keep and many questions remain unanswered. It is more like *A Dream Play* than we first realise, with striking shifts of time and place.[16]

Some interesting casting choices helped to convey the director's vision of the play. Turpin, who had directed *A Dream Play* in the previous season at the Theatre Academy in Stockholm, alluded to parallels between the two plays by casting actress Sara Turpin as the Student and thus making the character a counterpart of Indra's Daughter, who finds a path through the darkness of this shadow world.[17] The celebrated elderly opera singers Erik Saendén as the Old Man and Margareta Hallin as the Mummy were asked to play the main roles for their strong stage presence.[18] While the director seemed to share the general view that *The Ghost Sonata* exposes the lies and crimes of a corrupt and festering urban upper class, in the interview he noted what he felt was the play's twisted view on class. For him, 'One of its hugely traumatic features is that the servants are such monsters.'[19] By contrast, in Turpin's production the Cook (Thomas Köhler) was treated as a farcical character rather than a hideous vampire. Critics appreciated the humour he and other performers brought to the gloomy universe of the play.[20]

Each production element reinforced the ghost theme in order to create a kind of dream world, 'a dark mirror to *A Dream Play*', the director said.[21] Lars Östbergh designed an expressionistic set with distorted perspective. Doors and windows were cut in the backwards-leaning walls of white canvas stretched on wooden frames that enclosed the playing area. The turns of the revolving stage were coordinated with the performers' entrances and exits through a pair of doors, which reminded one reviewer of a giant clockwork[22] where statues of allegorical figures would glide around at regular intervals, appearing in one door and vanishing through the other, marking the cycles of life – in this case, of death. The occasional red blaze emitted by the backdrop intensified a sense of a grotesque dance of death, and a gigantic bird-cage for the parrot-Mummy in Act II created a hellish effect of a torture chamber. The same set remained standing throughout the performance, but in the second tableau (the 'round salon') hunting trophies – horns on bare animal skulls – adorned the walls. They provided an eerie parallel with the characters' spooky appearances and served as an allusion to the process of unmasking that took place in that room.[23] The theatre's architecture contributed to the intimate closeness of the spectators to the world of the performance, since the Intimate Theatre's new stage is surrounded in a semicircle by the rows of seats of the small auditorium.

The uncanny effect of the set was enhanced by the white make-up designed by Eva Faegne, featuring blackened eyes and vampire teeth, worn by every character but the Student. The figures looked like lifeless shadows from hell, indistinguishable even from the marble statue on the stage. The Student was the only character that retained a clear sense of humanity, wandering among the ghosts without make-up, as his true self. Played 'as a rebellious teenager nearly in despair',[24] he 'looked like the truth in a pandemonium of deceitful shams'.[25] Dror Feiler's music combined Wagner with a one-person orchestra, positioned at stage right outside the circle of the revolving stage, playing live music in the manner of a silent-movie setting. The emphasis on the ghost theme, the stylised performance combined with the expressionistic set, the exaggerated make-up, and the music linked the performance to the German silent cinema of the 1920s – such as *Nosferatu* and *The Cabinet of Doctor Caligari* – which, according to Turpin, was strongly influenced by Strindberg in its reaction against realism.[26]

The tone of the reception has changed significantly over the past century. Whereas reviewers of the 1908 production rejected the play as unfitting for the stage precisely because of its bizarre, unrealistic, and dream-like qualities, it was now celebrated as a text whose very essence is a 'ghostly absurdism'.[27] 'Here we have a fully developed absurdism almost half a century before the theatre invented absurdist drama,' declared Curt Bladh, while others simply called *The Ghost Sonata* Strindberg's absurdist play.[28] This time the performance received unanimous critical praise and reviewers regarded it as clearly 'Strindbergian'. Curt Bladh felt that Turpin's production was so powerful, while creating a sense of intrusive closeness with the audience, that it came close to 'what Strindberg and Falck, in their time … intended for a modern theatre'.[29] Nils Schwartz also believed that Turpin and his ensemble realised the spirit and style of performance envisioned by Strindberg: 'He would be in seventh heaven had he the opportunity to see the old opera singers Erik Saendén and Margareta Hallin as the Old Man … and the Mummy in this performance.'[30]

Reviewers' invocation of Strindberg's spirit upon experiencing the centennial production of *The Ghost Sonata* provides a fitting closure for this study that has set out to explore the dramatist's significance for the theatre, including the elaborate stagings of his life in the context of the political, social, and cultural scenes of European modernity and his involvement with the shaping of the discourses of theatre during his lifetime and beyond. In his book *The Haunted Stage*, theatre scholar Marvin Carlson proposes the concept of 'ghosting' as central to the theatrical experience historically. According to this view the complex recycling of texts, spaces, bodies, and other elements of theatrical performance culminates in an awareness not of similarity, but of identity, of what had been experienced before, which haunts and affects the meanings construed by the current experience (Carlson 2001: 6–7). Dramatic texts, as staged again and again in the theatre, become sites for 'storage and mechanism for the continued recirculation of cultural memory' (Carlson 2001: 8). Recycling, says Carlson,

> often serves to call the attention of the audience to the con-
> structedness of the theatrical performance. … A practice that in
> the past was … always springing from the deeper entanglement
> of theatre itself with the operations of individual and social
> memory, has appeared with new power, new prominence, and
> new motivations today.
>
> (Carlson 2001: 173)

Whether on the tiny stage rented by a former gas clerk in late-nineteenth-century Paris or at the state-of the-art National Theatre in London; whether with *Vasasagan* in Malmö, *Miss Julie* in Cape

Town, or *The Ghost Sonata* in New York, Strindberg both haunts
our cultural memory and continues to be a living presence worldwide
in the theatre of our day.

Notes

1 *Nya Dagligt Allehanda*, 11 January 1908, quoted in Bark 1981: 88.
2 Ibid.
3 *Stockholms Dagblad*, 21 January 1908, quoted in Bark 1981: 88.
4 *Dagens Nyheter*, 22 January 1902, quoted in Marker and Marker
  2002: 119.
5 *Stockholms Tidningen*, 22 January 1908, quoted in Bark 1981: 89.
6 *Göteborgs-Posten*, 5 May 1917, quoted in Bark 1981: 113.
7 *Nya Dagligt Allehanda*, 4 May 1917, quoted in Marker and Marker
  2002: 122.
8 *Stockholms Tidningen*, 4 May 1917, quoted in Bark 1981: 111.
9 Several photographs were published in the *Theatre Arts Monthly* (8
  April 1924). See reproductions in Stockenström 1988: xi.
10 'Spook Sonata, "Milestone in the Dramatic Season in New York"',
  Pennsylvania Register, 9 January 1924 and Alexander Wolcott, 'The
  Play', *New York Times*, 8 January 1924, quoted in Stockenström 1988:
  x–xii.
11 *Stockholms Tidningen*, 17 October 1942, quoted in Marker and Marker
  2002: 133.
12 For Egil Törnqvist's rehearsal diary and a transcription of the entire
  production in Swedish see Törnqvist 1973.
13 13 February 2000, quoted in Steene 2005: 752.
14 Per Theil, *Berlingske Tidende*, 14 February 2000, quoted in Steene 2005:
  752.
15 Lena S. Karlsson, 'Strindberg spökar på Stockholms scener', *Tidningen
  Kulturen*, 28 February 2008; www.tidningkulkturen.se/content/view/
  2573/128/ (accessed 18 September 2008).
16 Betty Skawonius, 'Turpin hyllar Strindberg på Intiman', *Dagens Nyheter*,
  3 December 2007; www.dn.se/kultur-noje/scen/turpin-hyllar-strindberg-pa-
  intiman-1.735891 (accessed 5 February 2009).
17 Nils Schwarts, 'Strindbergs intima teater/Spöksonaten', *Expressen*,
  8 December 2007; www.expressen.se/kultur/nilsschwartz/1.960319/strind-
  bergs-intima-teater-spoksonaten (accessed 5 February 2009).
18 Skawonius, 'Turpin hyllar Strindberg på Intiman'.
19 Ibid.
20 Karlsson, 'Strindberg spökar'; Claes Wahlin, 'Osaliga Andar', *Aftonbladet*, 8 December 2007; www.aftonbladet.se/kultur/article1426171.ab
  (accessed 5 February 2009).

21 Skawonius, 'Turpin hyllar Strindberg på Intiman'.
22 Schwarts, 'Strindbergs intima teater/Spöksonaten'.
23 Wahlin, 'Osaliga Andar'.
24 Curt Bladh, 'Spöksonat på Strindbergs vis', *Sundsvalls Tidning*, 9 December 2008; www.st.nu/noje/kultur.php?action=visa-artikel&id= 691771 (accessed 5 February 2009).
25 Schwarts, 'Strindbergs intima teater/Spöksonaten'.
26 Skawonius, 'Turpin hyllar Strindberg på Intiman'.
27 Bladh, 'Spöksonat på Strindbergs vis'.
28 Ibid.; and Andreas Jakobsson, 'Strindbergs teater 100 år', *Upsala Nya Tidning*, 2 December 2007; www2.unt.se/printartikel/1,3110,MC=5-AV-ID+697759-SC-ID+152,00.html (accessed 5 February 2009).
29 Bladh, 'Spöksonat på Strindbergs vis'.
30 Schwarts, 'Strindbergs intima teater/Spöksonaten'.

List of play titles and English translations

1899	*Folkungasagan*
	The Saga of the Folkungs
1899	*Gustav Vasa*
1899	*Erik XIV*
	Eric XIV
1900	*Gustav Adolf*
1900	*Midsommar*
	Midsummer
1900	*Kaspers fettisdag*
	Casper's Shrove Tuesday
1900	*Påsk*
	Easter
1900	*Dödsdansen* I, II
	The Dance of Death I, II
1901	*Kronbruden*
	The Crown Bride
1901	*Svanevit*
	Swanwhite
1901	*Carl XII*
	Charles XII
1901	*Till Damaskus* III
	To Damascus III
1901	*Engelbrekt*
1901	*Kristina*
	Queen Christina
1901	*Ett drömspel*
	A Dream Play (Prologue added in1906)
1902	*Gustav III*
1902	*Holländarn*
	The Flying Dutchman
1903	*Näktergalen i Wittemberg*
	The Nightingale of Wittenberg
1903	*Moses*
1903	*Sokrates*
	Socrates
1903	*Kristus*
	Christ

Bibliography

Antoine, A. (1964) *Memories of the Théâtre-Libre*, trans. M. Carlson, ed. H. D. Albright, Coral Gables, Florida: University of Miami Press.

Artaud, A. (1971) *Collected Works*, vol. 2, trans. V. Corti, London: Calder & Boyars.

——(1988) *Selected Writings*, trans. H. Weaver, ed. S. Sontag, Berkeley: University of California Press.

Bark, R. (1981) *Strindbergs drömspelteknik i drama och teater*, Lund: Studentlitteratur.

Barnett, D. (2005) *Rainer Werner Fassbinder and the German Theatre*, Cambridge: Cambridge University Press.

Beijer, A. (1954) *Teaterrecensioner 1925–1949 jämte en översikt av teater och drama i Sverige under seklets förra hälft*, Stockholm: Föreningen Drottningholmsteaterns Vänner.

Bergman, G. M. (1967) 'Strindberg and the Intima Teatern', *Theatre Research International* 9 (1): 14–47.

Brandell, G. (1974) *Strindberg in Inferno*, trans. B. Jacobs, Cambridge, MA: Harvard University Press.

——(1983–89) *Strindberg – Ett författarliv*, 4 vols, Stockholm: Alba.

Breton, A. (1978) *What is Surrealism? Selected writings*, ed. F. Rosemont, New York: Pathfinder Press.

Burian, J. (1971) *The Scenography of Josef Svoboda*, Middletown, CT: Wesleyan University Press.

——(1980) '*The Dream Play*, by August Strindberg', typewritten note, Jarka M. Burian Papers, University at Albany Libraries.

Carlson, H. G. (1982) *Strindberg and the Poetry of Myth*, Berkeley: University of California Press.

——(1996) *Out of Inferno: Strindberg's reawakening as an artist*, Seattle: University of Washington Press.

Carlson, M. (2001) *The Haunted Stage: The theatre as memory machine*, Ann Arbor: University of Michigan Press.

Cate, P. D. and Shaw, M. (eds) (1996) *The Spirit of Montmartre: Cabarets, humor and the avant-garde, 1875–1905*, New Brunswick, New Jersey: Rutgers University Press.

Ciaravolo, M. (2009) 'The Voice of the Lower Class in Strindberg's Swedish Historical Plays', *North-West Passage* 6: 151–77.

Croall, J. (2005) A Dream Play *Background Pack*, London: National Theatre Education; www.nationaltheatre.org.uk (accessed 25 April 2008).

Cullberg, J. (1992) *Skaparkriser: Strindbergs Inferno och Dagermans*, Stockholm: Natur och Kultur.

Dasgupta, G. (2001) 'The Hopeless Dream of "Being": Ingmar Bergman's *The Ghost Sonata*', *PAJ* (69): 86–91.

Deak, F. (1993) *Symbolist Theater: The formation of an avant-garde*, Baltimore and London: Johns Hopkins University Press.

Deutsch, H. and Hanau, S. (1972) *The Provincetown: A story of the theatre*, 1931 edition reissued, New York: Russel & Russel.

Eklund, T. (1948) *Tjänstekvinnans son: En psykologisk Strindbergsstudie*, Stockholm: Bonnier.

Fahlgren, M. (1994a) 'Kristina – The Public Woman', in K. Kvam (ed.) *Strindberg's Post-Inferno Plays*, Copenhagen: Munksgaard/Rosinante.

——(1994b) *Kvinnans ekvation: Kön, makt och rationalitet i Strindbergs författarskap*, Stockholm: Carlssons Förlag.

Frye, R. (1997) '*Miss Julie*', *Theatre Journal* 49 (4): 532–34.

Gerould, D. (ed.) (2000) *Theatre/Theory/Theatre: The major cultural texts from Aristotle to Soyinka and Havel*, New York: Applause Books.

Gray, S. (1985) 'Desegregating the theatre', *Index on Censorship* 14 (4): 11–17; http://dx.doi.org/10.1080/03064228508533915 (accessed 7 October 2008).

Hedvall, Y. (1923) *Strindberg på Stockholmsscenen 1870–1922: En teaterhistorisk översikt*, Stockholm: N. S. Lundströms Förlag.

Hegel, G. W. F. (1988) *Introduction to 'The Philosophy of History'*, trans. L. Rauch, Indianapolis: Hackett.

Hockenjos, V. (2001) 'The World Through a Panorama Lens: Strindberg on vision and visual technologies', in G. Rossholm, B. S. Sjönell and B. Westin (eds) *Strindberg and Fiction*, Stockholm: Almqvist & Wiksell International.

Huber, O. and Stückl, C. (2000) *The Passion Play: 2000, Oberammergau*, Munich and New York: Prestel.

Innes, C. (1993) *Avant-Garde Theatre, 1892–1992*, London: Routledge.

Jannarone, K. (2005) 'The Theatre before Its Double: Artaud directs in the Alfred Jarry Theatre', *Theatre Survey* 46 (2): 247–73.

Järv, H. (1981) 'Den Reaktionära radikalen' in *Strindberg*, Stockholm: Kulturhuset.

Jaspers, K. (1977) *Strindberg and Van Gogh: An attempt of a pathographic analysis with reference to parallel cases of Swedenborg and Hölderlin*, Tucson: University of Arizona Press.

Johnson, W. (1963) *Strindberg and the Historical Drama*, Seattle: University of Washington Press.

Knapp, B. L. (1988) *The Reign of the Theatrical Director: French theatre, 1887–1924*, Troy, NY: Whitson Publishing Company.

Kritzer, A. H. (2005) '*A Dream Play*', *Theatre Journal*, 57 (3): 502–4.

Kvam, K. (1974) *Max Reinhardt og Strindbergs visionære dramatik*, København: Akademisk forlag.

——(1991) 'Strindberg and French Symbolist Theatre', in M. Robinson (ed.) *Strindberg: The Moscow Papers*, Stockholm: Strindbergssällskapet.

Lagercrantz, O. (1984) *August Strindberg*, trans. A. Hollo, New York: Farrar, Straus & Giroux.

Lamm, M. (1924, 1926) *Strindbergs dramer*, vols 1–2, Stockholm: Bonnier.

——(1936) *Strindberg och makterna*, Stockholm: Svenska kyrkans diakonstyrelses bokförlag.

——(1971) *August Strindberg*, trans. H. G. Carlson, New York: Benjamin Blom.

Laurin, C. G. (1914) *Ros och ris: Från Stockholms teatrar 1903–13*, Stockholm: Norstedt.

Leach, G. (1986) *South Africa: No easy path to peace*, London: Routledge & Kegan Paul.

Lide, B. (1998) 'Strindberg på scenen idag: Postmoderna parodier', *Strindbergiana*, vol. 13: 82–91.

Lindström, H. (1952) *Hjärnornas kamp: Psykologiska idéer och motiv i Strindbergs åttiotalsdiktning*, Uppsala: Appelbergs boktryckeri AB.

Marker, L. and Marker, F. J. (eds) (1999) *Ingmar Bergman: A project for the theatre*, New York: Continuum.

——(2002) *Strindberg and Modernist Theatre: Post-Inferno drama on the stage*, Cambridge: Cambridge University Press.

Meyer, M. (1985) *Strindberg*, New York: Random House.

Miller, A. I. (1931) *The Independent Theatre in Europe, 1887 to the Present*, New York, B. Bloom.

Monié, K. (1981) 'Kvinnosyn in dikt och verklighet', *Strindberg*, Stockholm: Kulturhuset.

Myrdal, J. (2000) *Johan August Strindberg*, Stockholm: Natur och Kultur.

Ollén, G. (1961) *Strindbergs dramatik*, Stockholm: Sveriges Radio.

——(1972) *August Strindberg*, trans. P. Tirner, New York: Frederick Ungar.

Olsson, U. (2002a) '"Going Crazy": Strindberg and the construction of literary madness', in P. Houe, S. H. Rossel and G. Stockenström (eds) *August Strindberg and the Other: New critical approaches*, New York: Rodopi.

——(2002b) *Jag blir galen: Strindberg, vansinnet och vetenskapen*, Stockholm: Symposion.

Palmblad, H. V. (1927) *Strindberg's Conception of History*, New York: Columbia University Press.

Persson, A. (2004) *Vandra med August Strindberg: 12 vandringar i Stockholms skärgård*, Stockholm: Prisma.

Ranald, M. L. (1984) *The Eugene O'Neill Companion*, Westport, CT: Greenwood Press.

Rangström, T. (2007) 'Strindbergs Intima Teatern 100 år: Glimtar av teaterliv då och nu', *Strindbergiana,* vol. 22: 22–32.

Robinson, M. (1998) *Studies in Strindberg*, Norwich: Norvik Press.

Rosenqvist, C. (1994) 'Lepage: megastjärna i regi', *Dramat*, vol. 4: 31–34.

Rudnitsky, K. (1988) *Russian and Soviet Theater 1905–32*, trans. R. Permar, ed. L. Milne, New York: Harry N. Abrams.

Sauter, W., Martin, J. and Arntzen, K. O. (1993) 'Reactions on *Miss Julie*: The New Scandinavian Experimental Theatre's performance of *Miss Julie* in Copenhagen, 1992', 'Strindberg in Performance', Supplementary issue of *Theatre Research International*, vol. 18: *Nordic Theatre Studies* 6 (1–2): 3–10.

Savits, J. (1890) *Die Shakespeare-bühne in München*, Berlin: Druck von F. A. Günther & Sohn.

Schumacher, C. (ed.) (1996) *Naturalism and Symbolism in European Theatre 1850–1918*, Cambridge: Cambridge University Press.

——(2001) *Artaud on Theatre*, London: Methuen.

Scott, F. D. (1988) *Sweden: The nation's history*, Carbondale: Southern Illinois University Press.

Sellin, E. (1968) *The Dramatic Concepts of Antonin Artaud*, Chicago: University of Chicago Press.

Shideler, R. (1999) *Questioning the Father: From Darwin to Zola, Ibsen, Strindberg and Hardy*, Stanford, CA: Stanford University Press.

Short, H. P. (1910) *Oberammergau*, New York: Thomas Y. Crowell.

Showalter, E. (1985) *The Female Malady: Women, madness and English culture, 1830–1980*, New York: Pantheon Books.

Sjöberg, A. (1982) *Teater som besvärjelse: Artiklar från fem decennier*, Stockholm: P. A. Norstedt & Söners Förlag.

208   *Bibliography*

Smidig, B. (2006) 'Den stora mekanismen – I Holm/Møllers *Vasasagan*', Ph.D. dissertation, Lund: University of Lund, Mediatryck.

Sprinchorn, E. (1982) *Strindberg as Dramatist*, New Haven: Yale University Press.

Steene, B. (1992) 'Strindberg and History: An introduction' in B. Steene (ed.) *Strindberg and History*, Stockholm: Almqvist & Wiksell.

——(2005) *Ingmar Bergman: A reference guide*, Amsterdam: Amsterdam University Press.

Stockenström, G. (ed.) (1988) *Strindberg's Dramaturgy*, Minneapolis: University of Minnesota Press.

Strindberg, A. (1955) *Queen Christina – Charles XII – Gustav III*, trans. W. Johnson, Seattle: University of Washington Press.

——(1962) *The Chamber Plays*, 2nd edn, trans. E. Sprinchorn, S. Quinn and K. Petersen, Minneapolis: University of Minnesota Press.

——(1966a) *Open Letters to the Intimate Theater*, trans. W. Johnson, Seattle: University of Washington Press.

——(1966b) *The Son of a Servant: The story of the evolution of a human being*, trans. E. Sprinchorn, Garden City, New York: Doubleday Anchor Books.

——(1971a) *A Dream Play*, adapted by I. Bergman, trans. M. Meyer, New York: Dial Press.

——(1971b) *The Plays*, trans. M. Meyer, vol. 2, London: Secker & Warburg.

——(1972) *Getting Married*, trans. M. Sandbach, New York: Viking Press.

——(1979) *Plays of Confession and Therapy: To Damascus, I, II, III*, trans. W. Johnson, Seattle and London: University of Washington Press.

——(1984) *Fadren – Fröken Julie – Fordringsägare, August Strindbergs Samlade Verk*, vol. 27, Stockholm: Almqvist & Wiksell.

——(1988a) *Dödsdansen I–II, August Strindbergs Samlade Verk*, ed. L. Dahlbäck, vol. 44, Stockholm: Almqvist & Wiksell.

——(1988b) *Ett drömspel, August Strindbergs Samlade Verk*, ed. L. Dahlbäck, vol. 46, Stockholm: Almqvist & Wiksell.

——(1989) *Tjänstekvinnans son I–II, August Strindbergs Samlade Verk*, ed. L. Dahlbäck, vol. 20, Stockholm: Almqvist & Wiksell.

——(1991) *Kammarspel, August Strindbergs Samlade Verk*, ed. L. Dahlbäck, vol. 58, Stockholm: Almqvist & Wiksell.

——(1992) *Strindberg's Letters*, 2 vols, trans. M. Robinson, Chicago: University of Chicago Press.

——(1995) *Svarta fanor, August Strindbergs Samlade Verk*, ed. L. Dahlbäck, vol. 57, Stockholm: Almqvist & Wiksell.

——(1996) *Selected Essays*, trans. M. Robinson, Cambridge: Cambridge University Press.

——(1998) *Miss Julie and Other Plays*, trans. M. Robinson, Oxford: Oxford University Press.

——(2005) *A Dream Play*, adapted by C. Churchill based on a translation by C. Barslund, New York: TCG.

Swerling, A. (1971) *Strindberg's Impact in France 1920–1960*, Cambridge: Trinity Lane Press.

Szalczer, E. (2001) 'Nature's Dream Play: Modes of vision and Strindberg's re-definition of the theatre', *Theatre Journal* 53 (1): 33–52.

——(2008) *Writing Daughters: August Strindberg's other voices*, London: Norvik Press.

Szondi, P. (1987) *Theory of the Modern Drama*, trans. M. Hays, Minneapolis: University of Minnesota Press.

Törnqvist, E. (1973) *Bergman och Strindberg: Spöksonaten – drama och iscensättning, Dramaten 1973*, Stockholm: Prisma.

——(2000) *Strindberg's* The Ghost Sonata: *From text to performance*, Amsterdam: Amsterdam University Press.

Törnqvist, E. and Jacobs, B. (1988) *Strindberg's* Miss Julie: *A play and its transpositions*, Norwich: Norvik Press.

Uddgren, G. (1920) *Strindberg the Man*, trans. A. J. Uppwall, Boston: Four Seasons.

Uppwall, A. J. (1920) *August Strindberg: A psychoanalytic study with special reference to the Oedipus Complex*, New York: Haskell House.

Vivier, J. (2001) '*A Dream Play*', *Theatre Journal* 53 (3): 498–99.

Wainscott, R. H. (1997) *The Emergence of the Modern American Theater 1914–1929*, New Haven: Yale University Press.

Waxman, S. M. (1964) *Antoine and the Théâtre-Libre*, New York: Benjamin Bloom.

Wirmark, M. (1991) 'Strindberg's History Plays: Some reflections', in M. Robinson (ed.) *Strindberg and Genre*, Norwich: Norvik Press.

——(1994) 'Vakhtangov's Production of "Erik XIV", Moscow Art Theatre, First Studio, 1921', in K. Kvam (ed.) *Strindberg's Post-Inferno Plays*, Copenhagen: Munksgaard/Rosinante.

Index